POLICY STUDIES IN EMPLOYMENT AND WELFARE NUMBER 19

*General Editor: Sar A. Levitan*

# Employment and Earnings Inadequacy: A New Social Indicator

**Sar A. Levitan and Robert Taggart III**

The Johns Hopkins University Press, Baltimore and London

This study was funded by a grant from The Ford Foundation to The George Washington University Center for Manpower Policy Studies.

Manufactured in the United States of America

The Johns Hopkins University Press, Baltimore, Maryland 21218
The Johns Hopkins University Press Ltd., London

Library of Congress Catalog Card Number 74-6831
ISBN 0–8018–1623–8 (cloth)
ISBN 0–8018–1624–6 (paper)

The National Manpower Policy Task Force is a private non-profit organization of academicians who have a special interest and expertise in the area of manpower. The Task Force is primarily concerned with furthering research on manpower problems and assessing related policy issues. It sponsors three types of publications:

1. policy statements in which the Task Force members are actively involved as co-authors
2. studies commissioned by the Task Force and reviewed by a committee prior to publication
3. studies prepared by members of the Task Force, but not necessarily reviewed by other members.

Publications under Nos. 2 and 3 above do not necessarily represent the views of the Task Force or its members except those whose names appear on the study.

## Task Force Membership

# Contents

**List of Tables**

## List of Charts

**Preface**

The United States employment and unemployment statistics are as complete and sophisticated as any body of social data. They have been developed in response to a continually increasing demand for more detailed and dependable information about labor market behavior. With the aim of describing conditions in light of existing theories and policy concerns, these statistics have been refined, supplemented, and improved over the years.

The unemployment measure, for example, was first formulated and applied at the end of the Great Depression, when extensive and persistent joblessness could no longer be explained as a temporary adjustment phenomenon. New theories were emerging which argued that active governmental intervention was required to combat unemployment, and it was therefore vital to determine the number of idle people seeking work. The resulting unemployment measure was appropriate for assessing needs, since the majority of those displaced by the Depression were family heads with few alternative income sources other than earnings.

In subsequent decades, however, labor force composition and behavior changed. The stark consequences of interrupted employment were diminished by rising income, additional family earners, and support programs for the unemployed. Educational attainment became more critical, intensifying the structural labor market problems of the disadvantaged. In response, more detailed unemployment data were provided and supplementary statistics were introduced.

The thrust of this monograph is that cumulative changes in the economy and in labor market behavior have generated a need for a measurement which would consider the adequacy as well as availability of jobs which provide the income required for a minimally decent standard of living. An "Employment and Earnings Inadequacy" (EEI) index is proposed, and its conceptual strengths and weaknesses assessed. The index is calculated from data gathered by Current Population Surveys each March from 1968 through 1972. Using cross-sectional and longitudinal analysis, an attempt is made to determine how the components and the total vary by race, sex, family status, and area of residence, and how they fluctuate over the business cycle. The implications for several policy issues are then examined. The purpose is to demonstrate the feasibility and usefulness of an inadequacy measure, laying the groundwork for its implementation and utilization.

The EEI is another step in a long trend of development and analysis. Many persons contributed to the derivation of the subemployment concept on which it is based. In particular, Herman P. Miller worked with the authors of this monograph in developing the methodology used in this study.

A number of other experts have reviewed the manuscript. Without implicating them in the results, the critical comments and helpful contributions of the following are gratefully acknowledged: Seymour Brandwein, Howard Rosen, Burman Scrable, Robert Stein and James Wetzel, U. S. Department of Labor; Mollie Orshansky, U.S. Department of Health, Education and Welfare; Daniel Levine and Murray Weitzman, U.S. Department of Commerce; Betty Mahoney and Robert Raynsford, U.S. Office of Management and Budget; Courtenay Slater, Joint Economic Committee, U.S. Congress; Peter Henle, Congressional Research Service; Diane Sower and Joseph Zeisel, Federal Reserve Board; Harold Goldstein and W. Willard Wirtz, Manpower Institute;

James Bennett, Sheldon Haber, Charles Stewart, Theodore Unger, and Joyce Zickler. The George Washington University; Bennett Harrison, Massachusetts Institute of Technology; and Robert Aaron Gordon, University of California, Berkeley. Beverly Anderson prepared the manuscript for publication.

The study was prepared under a grant from The Ford Foundation to The George Washington University's Center for Manpower Policy Studies. In accordance with the foundation's practice, complete responsibility for the preparation of this volume was left to the authors.

Sar A. Levitan
Robert Taggart III

# 1

## Adapting Labor Market Statistics

Economic indices and statistics have become a familiar and vital part of everyday life, not merely describing reality, but having a major impact upon it. Social data affect perceptions of well-being, and thus the level of satisfaction or dissatisfaction. They also play a fundamental role in economic and social policymaking, since a variety of decisions by individuals, corporations, and public officials are based on regularly gathered and published statistics on everything from mortality and fertility to the sales of corn poppers and waffle irons. Such data have been generated to satisfy diverse informational needs. Their utility depends on their accuracy in describing reality, their clarity to users, and their usefulness to decisionmakers. Data needs are not immutable; as reality, theory, and applications change, measures must be added or adjusted in order to remain useful and accurate.

Labor market data are among the most detailed, dependable, and widely used U.S. government statistics. The President's Committee to Appraise Employment and Unemployment Statistics appointed by President Kennedy in 1961 put it succinctly:

It has been said that the seasonally adjusted unemployment rate is—at least in its political implications—the most important single statistic published by the Federal Government. Some may wish to temper the assertion with a caveat, but the detailed data on employment and unemployment now being reported by the Federal Government certainly constitute one of the major sources of economic intelligence available to the American people. As the President has stated in his charge to this committee: 'These statistics are of vital importance as measures of the economic health and well-being of the Nation. They serve as guides to public policy in the development of measures designed to strengthen the economy, to improve programs to re-employ the unemployed, and to provide assistance to those who remain unemployed.[1]

## Statistics in the Neoclassical Setting

"Unemployment," "employment," and "labor force participation" were neither defined, in the current sense, nor reliably measured until 1940. Prior to the Great Depression, prevailing economic theory denied the existence of any but temporary cyclical unemployment: workers without jobs were supposed to bid down the wage rate until all were employed for less pay. The annual average of two million unemployed during the 1920s was said to be the fault of individuals unwilling to accept lower wages, a step which economists believed would clear the market.

It took the massive dislocations of the 1930s to upset this neoclassical full-employment equilibrium theory and to force the government to adopt measures to aid the unemployed. With one of every four labor force participants unable to find a job in 1933—most of whom were previously stable workers—unemployment could not be written off as a temporary aberration. Yet, when President Roosevelt took office in 1933, there were no reliable measures of the extent of joblessness. The National Industrial Conference Board estimated that 2.9 million persons were unemployed in 1930, while WPA studies put the figure at 4.8 million.[2] According to the five most prominent estimates, unemployment in 1936 ranged between 5.4 and 8.1 million.[3]

[1]President's Committee to Appraise Employment and Unemployment Statistics, *Measuring Employment and Unemployment* (Washington: Government Printing Office, 1962), p. 9.

[2]Stanley Lebergott, *Manpower in Economic Growth* (New York: McGraw-Hill, Inc., 1964), p. 409.

[3]Paul Webbink, "Unemployment in the United States, 1930–1940," reprinted in U.S. Senate Subcommittee on Employment, Manpower and Poverty, *History of*

There had been no systematic efforts to measure the number of unemployed, and experts could not even agree on the definition of unemployment. In fact, until the 1930 Census the only systematic labor force data consisted of a "gainful workers" count recorded in each decennial Census. Individuals were asked what jobs they normally held when they worked. Those looking for work without previous job experience were not counted as unemployed, while those without jobs or employed in a different line of work were included as gainful workers in their usual occupation. This concept was designed to measure the productive work force rather than variations in employment or unemployment. The number of gainful workers could only increase by population growth, secularly increasing participation patterns, education, and other longer-run factors; it could only decline because of death, emigration, and delayed or diminished entry into the labor force.[4]

To estimate unemployment in any year, the number of gainful workers first had to be projected from decennial data. Estimates of employment then had to be derived from employer surveys. Unemployment was the difference between the two estimates. However, employer surveys were woefully inadequate, the decennial count of gainful workers was not very reliable (especially in counting female and younger workers), and projections for intercensal years were even more questionable. As an example, W. S. Woytinsky's March 1933 unemployment estimates were based on a projected demographic increase of 1.2 million gainful workers since 1930, and another increase of 1.9 million "additional workers" seeking jobs in order to make up for the unemployment of other family members.[5] There was a good deal of debate over this second adjustment. Clarence Long argued that the number of workers seeking jobs was not cyclically sensitive, and others questioned the concept of counting "additional workers" without previous experience as gainful employees.[6]

*Employment and Manpower Policy in the United States*, 88th Cong., 2nd Sess. (Washington: Government Printing Office, 1965), vol. 5, p. 2009.

[4]J. E. Morton, *On the Evolution of Manpower Statistics* (Kalamazoo, Michigan: The Upjohn Institute, 1969), pp. 36–51.

[5]Paul Webbink, "Unemployment in the United States," p. 2009.

[6]Clarence Long, *The Labor Force Under Changing Income and Employment* (Princeton, New Jersey: Princeton University Press, 1958).

Clearly, the gainful worker concept, with its underlying supposition that in the long run all those seeking jobs would be fully employed in their usual occupations, was not relevant in a depression setting. The critical issue was the number of people needing employment or relief assistance, not the size of the nation's human resource stock. Millions were willing and able to work but could not find jobs. What later became respectable Keynesian economic theory emerged as a pragmatic response to these conditions: first, the idea that unemployment could continue indefinitely; and second, the tenet that the government could and should alter the level of unemployment by its monetary and fiscal policies. During the New Deal, unemployment and old age insurance programs were initiated, along with massive job creation and relief efforts. These government programs, in turn, generated operational statistics and demands for additional data. Thus, the Great Depression necessitated a reexamination and revision of the earlier and rather limited labor market statistics.

## Employment and Unemployment Concepts

The current labor market concepts of unemployment, employment, and labor force participation were first defined and utilized at the end of the 1930s. The Works Progress Administration conducted a national post-card registration of the unemployed in 1937 and initiated a monthly household survey in 1939, first published in 1940. Three years later, this was transferred to the Census Bureau where sophisticated sampling techniques were implemented.[7] In these surveys, persons 14 years of age and over in the noninstitutional population were classified as either employed, unemployed, or not in the labor force. Employment and unemployment were the measured "status variables," with the labor force defined as the sum of the two, and the remainder of the population as not in the labor force. To be employed, the individual had to have worked for pay at least one hour during the last week, or for 15 hours without pay in a family enterprise. "Inactive workers" with jobs but not working because of illness, vacation, bad weather, a strike, or a

[7]J. E. Morton, *Manpower Statistics*, p. 55.

4

temporary (no more than 30-day) layoff, were included with the employed on the assumption that they had some job attachment.

This classification system differed significantly from the gainful worker concept. Where unemployment had previously been estimated by subtracting employer-reported employment from the estimated gainful work force, the new method measured unemployment directly and relied completely on the household response, with the work force being the derived statistic. Jobseekers without experience were not counted as gainful workers, but under the newer definitions, anyone looking for work would be counted as in the labor force.

These labor market definitions were not unequivocal. One issue was their dependence on a household member's subjective assessment of willingness and ability to work. Increased access to jobs, higher wages, or lower non-wage incomes could be expected to increase the desire to hold a job, consequently affecting reported levels of unemployment, even under improving labor market conditions.[8]

These problems of objective measurement were especially critical for secondary earners. To the extent that their incomes were not vital for their families' survival, wives and teenagers might easily be discouraged by bad times. On the other hand, other family members might seek work if the head lost his or her job. The net changes in labor force participation for these "secondary" earners would thus be a balance between "discouraged" and "additional worker" effects.[9] To the extent that wives and teenagers enter and leave the work force with greater frequency, the bounds between unemployment and non-labor force participation would be increasingly obscured as their share of all participants rose. The meaning of unemployment would also be changed. Unemployed primary workers were mostly looking for full-time jobs, while many wives and dependents were seeking only part-time employment.[10]

[8]Clarence Long, *The Labor Force Under Changing Income*, pp. 395–400.

[9]W. S. Woytinsky, *Additional Workers and the Value of Unemployment In the Depression* (New York: Social Science Research Council, Pamphlet Series No. 1, 1940), pp. 1–26.

[10]Gertrude Bancroft, *The American Labor Force* (New York: John Wiley and Sons, 1958), p. 199.

Another issue was "hidden" unemployment. Workers employed part-time but wanting full-time jobs were counted as employed even if they worked only one hour. The worker doing a few odd jobs because of the shortage of full-time positions would, therefore, be included among the employed. Self-employment might also disguise unemployment; persons wanting wage-paying jobs might work in family enterprises, given no other options.

The employment measure also did not differentiate between adequate and substandard employment. Only hours and not types of work were considered; only the receipt of wages and not their level. A worker would be counted as employed even if he or she were skilled but working in an unskilled job, doing "make-work" or eking out a bare living despite full-time employment. These types of underemployment would presumably increase cyclically with unemployment, so that deviations from the full employment level of underemployment would represent an increment of need in addition to the unemployed.[11]

The gainful worker concept also had some advantages over the newer labor force definitions. At any point in time, there could be a number of potential workers with job experience not currently able or willing to work, but who might be drawn back into the labor force if jobs paying "adequate" wages were easily available, for example, the housewife who had left her job to stay at home with the children. The gainful worker measure would give a better estimate of the labor supply under full-employment and, by identifying normal rather than current occupations of workers, would yield better estimates of work force utilization and human resource stocks. Likewise, it might provide a better perspective for assessing economic growth potential.[12]

Despite these reservations, most analysts in the 1940 and 1950s considered the new labor market statistics appropriate for the time, or at least the best compromise between the alternatives. Except for some minor definitional changes in 1945, and some revisions in sampling techniques in 1943 and 1955, the concepts insti-

[11]Paul Samuelson and Russell Nixon, "Estimates of Unemployment in the United States, *Review of Economics and Statistics*, August 1940, pp. 101–111.

[12]League of Nations, *Statistics of Gainfully Occupied Population*, Studies and Reports on Statistical Methods, Number 1 (Geneva, Switzerland: The League, 1938), p. 9.

tuted in the 1940 Census were utilized throughout the next two decades.

## A Reexamination

Public concern with the definition and derivation of the labor market statistics depended on the news they conveyed. As the President's Committee put it:

Public and academic discussion and criticism of the series understandably tend to increase during recessions, and some segments of the public have been reluctant to accept the recorded rise in unemployment as genuine. When recorded unemployment rises by an uncomfortable amount, some observers hasten to remind the public that the official count of the unemployed includes many people not actually in need or requiring public help, and the cry is raised in some quarters that these should be excluded. On the other hand, there are always complaints that the figures fail to reveal the real magnitude of unemployment problems—for example, the numbers who become discouraged and leave the labor force entirely, those on shorter hours, or the underemployed.[13]

The sluggish decline in unemployment from the 1958 peak generated a good deal of criticism of the unemployment concept, ranging from serious technical assessments seeking to improve the quality of the data to "purple prose" attacks questioning the value of the statistics. The Joint Economic Committee issued analyses of frictional and structural unemployment in 1959 and 1960, and another on employment concepts in 1961.[14] At the other extreme, a *Reader's Digest* article attacked the data and the gatherers, asserting that unemployment figures were more a creation of government bureaucrats than a reflection of real economic conditions.[15]

---

[13]President's Committee to Appraise Employment and Unemployment Statistics, p. 32.

[14]U.S. Congress, Joint Economic Committee, *The Extent and Nature of Frictional Unemployment*, 86th cong., 1st sess. (Washington: Government Printing Office, 1959); and *The Structure of Unemployment In Areas of Substantial Labor Surplus*, 86th cong., 2nd sess. (Washington: Government Printing Office, 1960); and *Unemployment: Terminology, Measurement, and Analysis*, Subcommittee on Economic Statistics, 87th cong., 1st sess. (Washington: Government Printing Office, 1961).

[15]James Daniel, "Let's Look at Those Alarming Unemployment Figures," *Reader's Digest*, September 1961, pp. 67–71.

But more was involved than a technical debate over the realism of unemployment estimates. Important changes had occurred in the labor market and new theoretical perspectives and public policy issues had emerged over the two decades since the labor market statistics were introduced. The question was not only whether labor market statistics were embarrassing in the slow recovery from a recession, but also whether they were appropriate after twenty years of change.

One major development was the increase in secondary workers. Female labor force participation, which rose dramatically in World War II, continued upward through the 1950s. Though the products of the post-war baby boom had not entered the labor force by 1960, structural changes were occurring, intensifying the relative unemployment problems of teenagers. The average unemployment rate of youths aged 16 to 19 years rose from 2.3 times the overall rate in 1950 to 2.7 times as high in 1960. In 1954, males age 20 years and over accounted for 65 percent of the labor force and 58 percent of the unemployed. By 1960, when the annual unemployment rate was the same, these adult males represented only 62 percent of the labor force and 54 percent of the unemployed.

Another development in the late 1950s was an apparent acceleration of technological change. "Disemployment," which was defined as the decline in production worker manhours associated with productivity advance, was twice as high, on the average, between 1957 and 1961 as between 1947 and 1957.[16] The impacts were concentrated geographically as well as socially—among the less educated—intensifying structural problems in the match-up of labor supply and demand. Depressed areas were an increasing concern, since between March 1953 and 1961, the number of communities counted as "economically distressed" rose from 35 to 285.[17]

---

[16]National Commission on Technology, Automation, and Economic Progress, *The Employment Impact of Technological Change*, Vol. II (Washington: Government Printing Office, 1966), p. 11; and Edwin Mansfield, "Technological Change: Measurement Determinants and Differences," p. 109.

[17]U.S. Congress, House Committee on Education and Labor, *Unemployment and the Impact of Automation*, 87th cong., 1st sess. (Washington: Government Printing Office, 1961), pp. 193, 380.

Another structural problem was the increasing disparity between the unemployment rates of whites and blacks. In 1948, the unemployment rate for nonwhites was 1.7 times that for whites. It rose to 2.0 times as high in 1954, and 2.2 times by 1959. The major factor in this increase was the exodus of rural and frequently underemployed blacks to the cities, where they became more visible as unemployed and where they also came into direct and uneven competition with whites for available jobs.

It was also becoming apparent in the late 1950s that millions of workers, in addition to the blacks and the technologically displaced, were unable to earn an adequate livelihood. Poverty was not new, but it remained to be "discovered." As with unemployment three decades earlier, there were no dependable statistics on poverty and standards for its measurement varied. It was not until 1964 that Mollie Orshansky of the Social Security Administration developed a generally accepted poverty index, but there were several approximations in the late 1950s and the first years of the 1960s which highlighted the problems.[18]

These developments were paralleled by changing public policy concerns. In the late 1950s, several youth employment and training bills were introduced. Area development legislation was proposed to help distressed communities, and manpower training was suggested for the technologically displaced. These became a reality with the passage of the Area Redevelopment and Manpower Development and Training Acts in the early 1960s, which also saw increased pressure for civil rights legislation, and mounting concern over poverty.

At the same time, labor market theories were gradually changing from a macro to a micro level. It was recognized that monetary and fiscal policies alone could not solve all unemployment problems, and that the unemployed were heterogeneous. There was consequently a shift toward the structural and institutional perspectives—"from mass to class unemployment."[19] Active labor

---

[18]Herman P. Miller, "The Dimensions of Poverty," in *Poverty As A Public Issue*, ed. Ben Seligman (New York: The Free Press, 1965), pp. 20–50.

[19]John T. Dunlop, "Public Policy and Unemployment," in U.S. Congress, Senate Special Committee on Unemployment Problems, *Studies in Unemployment*, 86th cong., 2nd sess. (Washington: Government Printing Office, 1960), pp. 1–16.

market policies were prescribed to reduce inequalities between individuals and areas.

Reacting to public criticism over the integrity of labor force data, President Kennedy appointed a blue-ribbon committee chaired by Professor Robert Aaron Gordon to appraise their dependability. But in light of the longer-run changes which had occurred, the Gordon committee interpreted its mission broadly: to assess not only the techniques of data gathering, but also the underlying concepts and definitions. The committee recommended an expansion of the household sample, analyzed the comparability of the household and employer surveys and unemployment insurance data, and discussed methods for better dissemination of information. More important, however, it gave careful consideration to the conceptual issues which had been raised earlier about such things as reliance on the self-assessment of willingness and ability to work, the extent of hidden unemployment and underemployment, and the implications of increasing labor force participation by women and teenagers. The question was whether changes in labor market conditions, theories, and policy concerns warranted changes in the labor market measures, particularly the unemployment rate. The committee sought to establish or modify concepts so that the resulting measures would be objective, operationally feasible, easily understood, and not overly inclusive.[20]

The result of this assessment was the judgment that the unemployment rate should be "purified" as a measure of the inability of active jobseekers to find work, rather than trying to merge it with other concepts to make it a measure of employment adequacy or of the total number of persons failing in or being failed by the labor market. Although the committee did not specifically recommend the exclusion of youths 14 to 15 years of age from the labor force, it did suggest that their inclusion raised problems since most of these youths had only marginal attachments to work and their opportunities were circumscribed by compulsory school attendance and child labor laws. The committee recommended that only workers with specific job-seeking activity within a prescribed period of time be counted as unemployed, and that those wanting

[20]President's Committee to Appraise Employment and Unemployment Statistics, p. 43.

jobs but not looking, including those discouraged by the unavailability of work, be counted as not in the labor force. Additional survey questions were suggested to provide objective criteria for judging whether actual jobseeking efforts had taken place. Proposals to limit those counted as unemployed to family breadwinners, to exclude the short-term unemployed, or to count as not in the labor force persons on layoff waiting to be called back to a job were discussed but eschewed.

While recommending only slight modifications to increase the objectivity and rigor of the unemployment measure, the Gordon committee urged that supplementary statistics be gathered and published on a regular basis. To assess the issue of increasing secondary workers, the committee proposed that data be added on full-time or part-time jobseeking intentions of the unemployed, and also on their family status. More information was also recommended on the reasons for unemployment. To assess discouragement, questions were recommended for persons not in the labor force, their current job interest, and their reasons for not working or looking for work. The committee did not have any recommendations concerning critical problems such as underemployment and the relationship between family and labor market status; it simply urged that more information be provided. The issue of the adequacy of earnings was virtually ignored.

The Bureau of Labor Statistics implemented most of the Gordon committee recommendations. The household survey sample was expanded in 1967 from 35,000 households in 357 areas to 50,000 in 449 areas, permitting more detailed reporting of personal and geographic characteristics. The unemployment concept was modified to make it a more rigorous measure of active job searching, while new statistical series were developed to shed light on other aspects of labor market behavior:

1. The unemployment definition was tightened to include only individuals who had taken specific steps within the previous four weeks to look for a job and who were currently available for work. Inactive jobseekers who have quit looking because of the lack of opportunities, and students seeking summer jobs before the end of the school year, were no longer counted as unemployed.

2. The labor force was redefined to include only individuals age 16 years of age and over, excluding persons 14 to 15 years of age from regular employment and unemployment figures.

3. Persons holding a job but not at work who were looking for other employment were classified as employed.

4. Most of the labor market statistics were subclassified by household status permitting a differentiation between primary and secondary workers.

5. A number of questions were added to determine the activities and behavior of nonlabor force participants. They were asked their intentions to seek work in the next year, whether they wanted a job, if so why they were not looking, and when and why they had left their past position.[21]

## The Subemployment Concept

While these refinements and additions were useful, the scenario was much different by the time most of the Gordon committee's recommendations had been implemented in 1967. One significant change was the flood of the post-war baby boom generation into the labor market. In 1960, youths from 16 to 19 years of age constituted 7.3 percent of the labor force; by 1967, they accounted for 8.8 percent. More strikingly, the teenage labor force grew by 35 percent, or more than three times the rate of the adult labor force. This influx intensified teenagers' relative unemployment problems. In 1960, their unemployment rate was 2.7 times the aggregate; by 1967, it was 3.4 times as high. The trend of increasing female participation in the labor force also continued; where males age 20 years and over represented 62 percent of the labor force in 1960, they were 59 percent in 1967.

The riots in Watts in 1965, followed by similar disturbances in other cities, focused attention on the structural labor market problems which had not been eliminated by a booming economy. The National Advisory Commission on Civil Disorders found that "more than 20 percent of the rioters in Detroit were unemployed,

---

[21]Robert L. Stein, "New Definitions for Employment and Unemployment," *Employment and Earnings*, February 1967, pp. 1–7.

and many who were employed held intermittent, low status, unskilled jobs which they regarded as below their education and ability." The conclusion was that "pervasive unemployment and under-employment are the most persistent and serious grievances of minority areas. They are inextricably linked to the problems of civil disorders."[22]

The War on Poverty under the Economic Opportunity Act of 1964 also focused attention on those at the end of the labor queue who continued to experience difficulties in a full employment economy. New data were gathered which, for the first time, detailed the characteristics of the poor. In 1966, when 6.1 million families were classified as poor, three of every five of these families were headed by a person with some work experience during the previous year. There were 1.9 million families which, in spite of the fact that their head worked full-time, full-year, remained in poverty. A healthy economy was a help but not a cure for the labor market problems of the disadvantaged.[23]

Yet, the overriding economic development of the 1960s was the sustained prosperity which produced "full employment" for most groups. Aggregate unemployment fell to 3.7 percent by the end of 1967. For white males 20 years of age and over, the rate fell to 1.9 percent in 1969, the lowest since World War II and close to the "irreducible" unemployment level compatable with mobile free labor markets. Although differentials for other groups remained, all (except black teenagers) benefitted.

With plentiful jobs, qualitative issues became more critical and attention focused on factors contributing to continued idleness in tight labor markets: the lack of commitment to work, the unavailability of transportation, hiring discrimination, and other structural impediments. An explanation was sought for the continuing employment and income problems of youths, minorities and ghetto residents.

In June 1966, President Lyndon Johnson directed the Department of Labor to conduct an intensive investigation to determine

---

[22]*Report of the National Advisory Commission on Civil Disorders* (Washington: Government Printing Office, 1968), p. 11.

[23]Mollie Orshansky, "The Shape of Poverty in 1966," *Social Security Bulletin*, March 1968, p. 14.

the characteristics of those who remained unemployed, where they were located, and why they were not working. Believing that unemployment was only one dimension of the labor market problems faced by the unskilled and poorly educated, especially those concentrated in ghetto areas, then-Secretary of Labor W. Willard Wirtz decided to explore a new concept which would measure not only unemployment, but also the adequacy of employment and earnings. The resulting "subemployment" measure included the following:

1. jobseekers counted as unemployed by the Current Population Survey definition;

2. individuals employed on a part-time basis but wanting to work full-time;

3. family heads with full-time jobs earning less than $60 weekly (the full-year wage needed at that time to raise a family of four above the poverty threshold) and unrelated individuals under age 65 years earning less than $56 weekly in full-time jobs (the then minimum hourly wage times 40);

4. half of all males 20 to 64 years of age who were not in the labor force—a rough estimate of discouraged workers who would presumably be active jobseekers if better opportunities were available; and

5. half the difference between the measured female and male adult populations—an adjustment for the undercount of the males missed by labor market surveys who might be expected to have the above problems.

Applying this measure to ten ghetto areas in eight major cities (Boston, New Orleans, New York, Philadelphia, Phoenix, San Antonio, San Francisco, and St. Louis), the Labor Department found that 34.7 percent of the adult population was subemployed, or, as Secretary Wirtz put it, "out of every three people in these slum areas who ought to be earning a living, one isn't."[24] The average unemployment in these ghettos was a disturbing 10.7 per-

[24] W. Willard Wirtz, "A report on Employment and Unemployment in Urban Slums and Ghettos: Memorandum For The President," December 23, 1966, in U.S. Congress, Senate Subcommittee on Employment, Manpower and Poverty, *Comprehensive Manpower Reform*, 92nd cong., 2nd sess. (Washington: Government Printing Office, 1972), Part 5, p. 2292.

cent, but this was clearly only the tip of the iceberg, with the other components accounting for two-thirds of the subemployed.

The assertion that a third of the central city ghetto adult population was failing in or being failed by the labor market became "official" when the subemployment findings were published in the 1967 *Manpower Report of the President.* But many could not accept so inclusive a measure of need, and technicians raised a number of valid criticisms of the definition:

1. One issue was the earnings standards of $60 weekly for full-time working family heads and the $56 weekly for unrelated individuals. While neither was especially generous, that for unrelated individuals was more inclusive since their poverty or minimum needs standard was roughly half that for a family of four. By using the earnings measure for a single survey week, the index excluded those whose low income resulted from intermittent employment. Many more workers experience unemployment during the course of the year than are unemployed at any point in time, and the fact that an individual is working at a point in time and earning $60 a week does not guarantee earnings above the poverty level.

2. The subemployment index did not differentiate uniformly between primary and secondary workers. While only family heads and unrelated individuals were counted in the earnings standards, wives and other relatives were included in the unemployed and part-time worker components of the subemployed. As a result, the count included some persons who may have been members of relatively affluent families.

3. The estimates of discouraged workers were open to question. There was no evidence that half of the males outside the labor force wanted to work and could not find jobs. In fact, a 1970 survey of 60 ghetto areas in 51 cities revealed that while 65 percent of males 22 years of age and over who were not in the labor force claimed they wanted to work, only an eighth of these listed the inability to find employment as either a primary or secondary reason for not looking. The survey also found that three times as many females as males were not in the labor force because of inability to find a job, and half of these discouraged women were

household heads.[25] Females should obviously have been included among discouraged workers.

4. The undercount correction was also questionable. Although unattached males were more likely to be missed by census enumerators than others, the adjustment factor used in subemployment calculations was too large. Also, attempts to determine the characteristics of undercounted males in central city areas through casual interviews have suggested that those missed have very similar labor force status to those who are counted.[26]

5. The subemployment concept was only applied to central city poverty neighborhoods. Because the aim was to demonstrate the concentration of employment problems, a high (and perhaps exaggerated) rate was predetermined by the choice of low-income areas with severe labor market problems. A national baseline was needed to determine the prevalence of such conditions elsewhere in the country.

Because of these conceptual shortcomings and because of its alarming implications, the subemployment index was disregarded by many technicians and policymakers. What should have been taken as a first effort toward the development of a new labor market measure was instead accepted at face value and used as a "scare index" to gain support for ghetto assistance programs. This instantaneous policy application was a setback to those trying to gain acceptance for the subemployment concept. Nevertheless, the 1967 subemployment estimates undeniably demonstrated that for particular groups in the population, low earnings and underemployment were even more serious problems than unemployment. Whether the specific index was acceptable, some measure which would combine the earnings, underemployment and unemployment concepts was clearly needed to assess the existing conditions for disadvantaged segments of the population.

Working to provide such a measure, the Labor Department published a national subemployment rate in the 1968 *Manpower*

---

[25]U.S. Bureau of the Census, Department of Commerce, *Employment Profiles of Selected Low-Income Areas*, Series PHC(3)-3 (Washington: Government Printing Office, 1972), pp. 64–66.

[26]Deborah P. Klein, "Determining the Labor Force Status of Men Missed in the Census," *Monthly Labor Review*, March 1970, pp. 28–30.

*Report of the President.* Based on more restrictive criteria than the ghetto index, it included all persons working full-time, full-year, but earning less than $3,000 annually, and those unemployed 15 or more weeks during the year. By this definition, a tenth of the labor force was subemployed in 1966, a decline from 17 percent in 1961. But significant differentials based on sex and race persisted.[27]

The differences between the two subemployment measures were significant. The ghetto index was based on the status of individuals in the survey week, and included those earning less than a weekly wage which, if maintained full-year, would raise a family of four out of poverty. The national index was based on earnings and work experience over the entire year. This was an important conceptual advance because it recognized that persistently low earnings and frequent or lengthy periods of unemployment were the real sources of distress, not the temporary unemployment which accompanied entrance and re-entrance into the labor force. However, the national index raised as many questions as it answered, and was extremely crude. It ignored the millions of low-wage earners working less than full-time, full-year, but with less than 15 weeks of unemployment; it made no adjustment for family income and no distinction between primary and secondary earners, and it did not include discouraged workers.

But the new subemployment measure was only proposed as a "rough, broad-guage indication of the proportion of workers with a substandard employment-earnings situation," and further modification and supplementation were urged. Endorsing the subemployment concept, the 1968 *Manpower Report* testified to the need for and value of such a measure:

The concept of subemployment reflects the judgment that workers with low earnings may have problems of as much concern from the viewpoint of manpower policy as those of many workers with substantial unemployment. The purpose of analyzing low earnings in conjunction with unemployment is not to equate the two, since they represent very different problems that will yield to very different solutions. Rather, the concept of subemployment is designed to provide a summary measure of the total

[27] *Manpower Report of the President, 1968* (Washington: Government Printing Office, 1968), p. 35.

problem of unemployment and low earnings, its compounded impact on the same disadvantaged groups, and its effects in preventing several million workers and their families from sharing in the Nation's economic prosperity.[28]

## Unemployment As An Overstatement of Need

When unemployment rose at the end of the 1960s, the disadvantaged had to compete with other groups who needed assistance, thus undercutting support for an index concentrating on the hardest core. The average number of unemployed persons rose from 2.8 million in 1969 to 5.0 million two years later, an increase which was felt by even the most "advantaged" groups in the labor force. The number of unemployed males 20 years of age and over more than doubled between 1969 and 1971, reaching 1.7 million. Priority was given to the normally steady workers forced into idleness and also to assisting returning veterans, who had transitional but less frequent or deeply-rooted problems. Persons at the end of the labor queue with more severe and persistent employment problems were given lesser priority.

With the rise in unemployment, labor market statistics were also questioned because of the bad news they bore. Gainsayers marshalled evidence that some of the unemployed were not really able or willing to work and that many of them had other sources of income. Diametrically, advocates of more help for the disadvantaged maintained that the existing labor market measures understated the problems, especially for the disadvantaged hit hardest by the recession.

Though this debate was not new in a slack economy, the arena in which it took place had been altered dramatically by changing economic and social conditions, concepts, and concerns in the late 1960s. The changing composition of the labor force was one of the most important developments. Labor force participation of women continued to increase. Adult males 20 years of age and over accounted for 65 percent of the work force in 1954, but only 56 percent in 1972. They represented 58 percent of the unemployed in 1954, but 40 percent in 1972. Alternatively, married males

[28] *Ibid.*, p. 34.

living with their wife accounted for 52 percent of those looking for or holding jobs in April 1947, and wives living with their husband just 11 percent. By March 1972, the married male segment had declined to 46 percent of the labor force while the working wives share doubled to 22 percent.

Some argued that changes in the composition of the work force had made it more difficult to achieve low levels of unemployment without high rates of inflation. Received labor market theory asserts that the rate of unemployment varies inversely with the rate of inflation: when unemployment is lower, wages rise faster because workers have more leverage and employers eagerly bid for scarce labor, which, in turn, raises prices more rapidly. Monetary and fiscal policies can only reduce the rate of inflation by easing labor market pressures and allowing unemployment to rise.

Some allege that there may have been changes in the underlying relationship between prices and unemployment caused by shifts in the labor force. If the proportion of the unemployed who are wives and teenagers seeking part-time work in trade or service occupations increases, rising unemployment does not relieve bottlenecks for skilled workers or undermine unions' ability to bargain for higher wages. Thus, with the growth of the "peripheral" work force, unemployment may have become less effective in alleviating labor shortages and pressure on wages and prices. Over the long run, the inflation-unemployment tradeoff may have been altered.

Weighting the unemployment rate by the "economic contribution" of each group of workers—using their earnings as a proxy for this contribution—permits an identification of the effects of compositional change. An index based on the average wages times manhours of work per week would give male workers 35 to 44 years of age six times the "weight" of teenage males.[29] Over the last decades, the weighted unemployment rate has risen by less than the measured rate, since the groups with low weights—teenagers and females—make up a growing share of the unemployed. The difference between the weighted and unweighted rates increased from a half of a percent in the late 1940s and early 1950s

[29]George L. Perry, *Inflation and Unemployment* (Washington: The Brookings Institution, 1970), p. 40.

to a full point in the late 1960s, making it more difficult to achieve full employment without an intolerable level of inflation.

Focusing on these increasingly difficult tradeoff problems, a study published by the Joint Economic Committee in 1973 projected that even under the most favorable conditions, the unemployment rate would remain over 4 percent in 1976, to a large extent because of the structure of unemployment. The study estimated that if adult male unemployment were reduced to 1.5 percent—lower than has been achieved in any post-war year—the projected rate for males 16 to 19 years of age would be 11.4 percent, for white females 20 years and over, 3.2 percent, and for nonwhite teenagers 24.5 percent.[30] The conclusion was that aggregate monetary and fiscal policies had little chance of achieving 4.0 percent unemployment. Apparently, this argument was accepted by policymakers in the early 1970s. Economic and budgetary actions demonstrated a willingness to accept a higher rate of unemployment as well as a reluctance to expand or implement efforts to ameliorate structural problems.

Another argument for accepting higher unemployment is that voluntary idleness can be weathered with greater ease now than in the past. With increased income, two or more earners in most families, and liberalized unemployment compensation and welfare, most of the unemployed can avoid breadlines and penury when earnings cease for a short period.

Rising income has undoubtedly provided a cushion for the unemployed. Between 1959 and 1971, real median family income rose by 37 percent. While it is true that today a family with only one earner may be no better off with its head unemployed than in the past, the majority of families have secondary earners or accumulated assets. Between 1960 and 1970, the proportion of husband-wife families with two or more labor force participants rose from 43 to 53 percent.

Various income maintenance programs also serve to cushion unemployment. Unemployment insurance is of the most direct importance, providing payments based on previous earnings to those who have acquired sufficient continuous employment to qualify

---

[30]Martin S. Feldstein, *Lowering the Rate of Unemployment*, a preliminary report prepared for the Joint Economic Committee. In Press.

for benefits. If there were no benefits, stark necessity would force the unemployed back to work more rapidly. There is little evidence, however, that changes in unemployment insurance over the past decade have led to changes in the behavior of the unemployed. While the number of insured workers has increased, the ratio of average annual beneficiaries to average annual unemployed declined from 43 to 36 percent between 1960 and 1971. But the benefits did not keep pace with the rising standard of living, so it is unlikely that more of the unemployed are "enticed" to malinger as unemployment beneficiaries now than a decade ago.

Another income maintenance program with an impact on work patterns is public assistance, specifically Aid to Families With Dependent Children. In 1960, there was an average of 0.8 million cases, affecting 2.1 million persons. By the end of 1972, the caseload had risen to over 3.1 million, with more than 11.0 million recipients. Over this period, the average monthly cash payment increased from $108 to $189, and added in-kind assistance raised AFDC benefits considerably higher. With liberalized eligibility criteria and increasing benefits, some of the AFDC growth represented persons choosing welfare over work or combining the two. In 1971, 9 percent of recipients were employed full-time, 6 percent part-time. There was also a high rate of turnover in the caseload with two-fifths of the cases being closed during 1970, sometimes because of earnings from work.[31]

It is difficult, however, to estimate the impact of welfare on measured unemployment and labor force participation rates, or its use as a cushion against unemployment. In 1971, 30 percent of married women living with their husbands who had children under 6 years of age were labor force participants, as were 49 percent of women with older children; only a fifth of welfare mothers were labor force participants, although another fifth had been in the labor force at some time in the preceding year. Some beneficiaries may be reluctant to seek jobs because of the welfare cushion, thus explaining some of the participation differentials. Most of the differentials, however, are explained by the employment handicaps characterizing welfare recipients. The unemployment rate of

[31]Sar Levitan, Martin Rein, and David Marwick, *Work and Welfare Go Together* (Baltimore: The Johns Hopkins University Press, 1973), pp. 49–55.

female heads of families with children under 6 years of age was 15 percent in March 1971, compared with 27 percent for welfare recipients. The aggregate effect on unemployment rates is unknown, however, since some unemployed mothers qualify for welfare and consequently withdraw from the labor force, while others may claim to be unemployed but do not accept jobs as long as welfare is available. The unemployed parent component of AFDC, under which male family heads can receive benefits, has remained small, with an average caseload of 150,000 in 1971, or only 3 percent of the average annual unemployed.

Other income maintenance programs, such as workmen's compensation and Social Security, as well as private retirement plans, influence labor market participation patterns and also cushion the impact of idleness. The latter two especially affect older workers who have been gaining increased options for complete retirement or at least reduced work.

Expanded income maintenance programs, rising income, and more frequent work by wives have important policy implications. The structuring of unemployment compensation benefits and payroll taxes must take into account any work disincentive effects. The potential and actual labor force status of welfare recipients must be considered in balancing work incentives and requirements with job creation efforts. Manpower programs and other policies to overcome structural problems must take into account the altering distribution of unemployment. But perhaps most important of all, the expansion of income alternatives to work has cushioned unemployment so that it is not as inimical to welfare as in the past; to some, this justifies a higher unemployment target for government economic policies.

### Unemployment As an Understatement of Need

Data gathered as a result of the implementation of the Gordon Committee's recommendations, and surveys of labor market conditions in a large number of ghetto areas from 1968 to 1970, provided documentation of severe problems not measured by the unemployment rate. First, the Bureau of Labor Statistics developed more accurate estimates of the number of discouraged workers. A variety of questions were added to the household survey in 1967. Persons not in the labor force were asked if they wanted a regular job, either full-time or part-time, and if so, why they were not looking. Discouraged workers were defined to include those currently wanting a job but not looking because they believed work was unavailable, lacked the skills or education demanded by employers, were too young or too old, or had other personal handicaps. Persons not in the labor force because of poor health, school attendance, or home responsibilities, were not included even if they wanted a job.

This measure is, of course, dependent on subjective self-assessment of work desires, and there is no way to determine the degree of impediments. The marginal cases are weeded out by the exclusion of those who are not sure they want a job and of those who are involved in other activities which prevent them from working or seeking work. Yet the measure is still based on an *attitude* rather than a demonstrated *commitment* or objectively identifiable *action*.

Nevertheless, five years of data on discouragement have demonstrated general year-to-year consistency. In 1967, there were 52.5 million persons in the civilian noninstitutional population 16 years of age and over who were not in the labor force, 4.7 million of whom claimed that they wanted a job. Eighty-five percent of these were in school, ill, disabled, or with family responsibilities, restricting their availability for work, leaving 732,000 who were counted as discouraged. During the tight labor markets of 1969, the number of discouraged workers fell to 574,000, and then climbed during the recession to 765,000 in 1972. Discouragement, is thus mildly correlated with unemployment.[32]

The discouraged worker is most frequently a "peripheral" labor market participant. In 1972, males accounted for less than a third of the total, and males 20 to 59 years of age, only an eighth. The majority of the discouraged had been out of the labor force for some time, with 31 percent having not worked for between one and five years, 19 percent for more than five, and 14 percent never

[32]Paul O. Flaim, "Discouraged Workers and Changes in Unemployment," *Monthly Labor Review*, March 1972, p. 11.

having worked. Yet, more than three-fourths of discouraged workers in 1972 indicated that they intended to look for a job within the next year.

Quite clearly, discouraged worker statistics do not measure the labor force reserve. In 1971, 8.3 million persons not in the labor force stated that they intended to look for work in the next year, compared with only 774,000 counted as discouraged.[33] The discouraged workers also do not fit the stereotype of those who are laid off and then give up because they cannot find reemployment; most are secondary workers who have not worked in the previous year. Thus, discouragement does not necessarily equate with economic distress. The individuals are being maintained in some way, mostly by the work of other family members or transfer payments. On the other hand, the statistics do provide a realistic measure of those who are frustrated in their job search or in their limited potential and are outside the labor force because of their feeling or knowledge that they cannot succeed.

Another type of hidden unemployment involves workers who hold part-time jobs (less than 35 hours weekly) but prefer full-time work. Roughly one in seven employed persons is a part-time worker. While this percentage increased in the past decade, the proportion employed part-time involuntarily because of the unavailability of full-time jobs declined:

|  | 1962 | 1972 |
|---|---|---|
| Part-time nonagricultural workers (millions) | 8.9 | 12.3 |
| Involuntary part-time for economic reasons (millions) | 2.4 | 2.4 |
| Percent female | 44 | 51 |
| Percent males under 25 or over 65 years | 18 | 23 |
| Percent males 25 to 64 years of age | 38 | 26 |

Although a growing majority of the involuntary part-time employees are secondary earners, many breadwinners are also affected adversely. In 1972, there were 626,000 males 25 to 64

[33]Jacob Mincer, "Determining Who are the 'Hidden' Unemployed," *Monthly Labor Review*, March 1972, p. 28.

years of age, most of whom were household heads, among the involuntary part-time nonagricultural workers.

Whether these persons should be given equal weight with the unemployed is open to debate. The job shortfall is roughly comparable for part-time workers seeking full-time jobs and for the fifth of the unemployed who only want part-time work. Also, it should be noted that some who are counted as part-time workers are normally full-time employees who have lost or left their jobs during the survey week. Unless their families have other sources of income, involuntary part-time-working family heads face severe economic problems since their jobs, on the average, pay less per hour than full-time work, with fewer hours meaning an even smaller weekly paycheck.

Discouraged, involuntary part-time, and unemployed workers together represent only a minority of those failing in or being failed by the economic system. In 1971, there were 2.8 million poor families whose head worked at some time during the year, and more than one million whose head worked full-time, full-year. A third of a million unrelated individuals were also fully employed but remained in poverty.[34]

These data understate the number of breadwinners failing in the labor market because they count combined family income rather than the income of the head. In April 1971, it is estimated that there were 5.8 million full-time and 5.3 million part-time jobs paying less than $2.00 per hour—the amount needed on a full-year basis to raise a family of four out of poverty.[35] While many of the workers in these jobs were secondary earners, their paycheck may still have been vital to lift the family out of poverty or to close the gap below. The labor market fails many millions in providing earnings which permit the maintenance of a family by a single breadwinner, and falls short in some cases where there are two or more earners.[36]

[34]U.S. Bureau of the Census, Department of Commerce, Current Population Reports, *Characteristics of the Low-Income Population, 1971*, Series P-60, No. 86, December 1972, table 13.
[35]Peter Henle, "The Dilemma of Low-Paid Jobs" (Washington: Brookings Institution, 1972, unpublished), table 1.
[36]Sar A. Levitan, *Programs In Aid of The Poor for the 1970s*, rev. ed. (Baltimore: The Johns Hopkins University Press, 1973), chapter 3.

Low earnings, unemployment, and other labor market problems are interrelated. Recent theories of the dual or segmented labor market focus on these interrelationships and the unfortunate consequences for the individuals affected. The dual labor market theory runs contrary to conventional or neoclassic notions that workers are paid according to their marginal productivity, that employers and individuals will invest in training to increase output, and that geographic and occupational mobility is unrestricted. Instead, this theory asserts that many workers are trapped in low-paying and unpromising jobs in a secondary labor market as a result of deficient education, discrimination and outright exploitation. Because of their limited options, such workers lack job commitment or long-range plans, and are frequently attracted to alternative income sources such as welfare or illicit activities. Employers of these unskilled workers expect high turnover, pay low wages, provide little training, and offer few opportunities for advancement.[37]

This segmented labor market theory obviously builds on earlier work. "Structuralists" have argued for some time that changes in the demand for labor have stranded groups of individuals. Theories of discrimination, economic development, education, and migration have all addressed similar issues. But the dual or segmented labor market hypothesis links these strands, attempting to demonstrate and interrelate the forces that cut workers off from the economic mainstream by cumulative and compounded effects which are not adequately considered in conventional economic theories or adequately addressed by existing labor market statistics.

### Resurrecting Subemployment

With its assertion that low earnings, unemployment, involuntary part-time work, and discouragement are linked causally for certain groups, the segmented labor market theory provided con-

---

[37]Bennett Harrison, *Education, Training, and the Urban Ghetto* (Baltimore: The Johns Hopkins University Press, 1972), pp. 117–52; and Peter B. Doeringer and Michael J. Piore, *Internal Labor Markets and Manpower Programs* (Lexington, Massachusetts; D. C. Heath, 1971), chapters 7, 8.

ceptual support for the reformulation of the subemployment measure. In 1970, the U.S. Bureau of the Census collected detailed labor market information in 60 poverty areas of 51 large cities. Based on questionnaires which had been tested and developed earlier in six large city poverty areas, the Census Employment Survey (CES) provided a detailed and relatively dependable statistical basis for assessing conditions in the nation's inner cities. Little effort was made by the Bureau of the Census and the Department of Labor to interpret and utilize these data. This task was left to the majority staff on the Senate Subcommittee on Employment, Manpower and Poverty, in conjunction with academic labor market economists, to utilize this information and to develop a new subemployment measure. The subcommittee's index, published in November 1972, included the following:

1. the unemployed,
2. those working part-time involuntarily for economic reasons,
3. individuals not in the labor force who wanted but were not seeking work because they did not think they could find employment, and
4. full-time workers paid less than $80 a week.[38]

Calculating this index from the poverty area data, the subcommittee found that 30.5 percent of the labor force was subemployed. Roughly an eighth of the subemployed were workers on part-time schedules for economic reasons, another eighth were discouraged workers, 30 percent were unemployed, and 45 percent were low earners.

This subemployment index and its application improved upon the 1967 work. The data base was broader and more reliable. The index made no adjustment for male undercount which, as indicated, was one of the more tenuous assumptions in the earlier calculations. The discouraged worker estimate was based on specific interview questions rather than "guesstimates" from labor

[38]U.S. Congress, Senate Subcommittee on Employment, Manpower and Poverty, "The Subemployment: 1970 Rates and Wirtz Memorandums," in *Comprehensive Manpower Reform*, 1972, Part 5, 92nd cong., 2nd sess. (Washington: Government Printing Office, April 1972), pp. 2276–80; and William Spring, Bennett Harrison, and Thomas Vietorisz, "Crisis of the Underemployed" *New York Times Magazine*, November 5, 1972, reprinted in *Comprehensive Manpower Reform*, 1972, pp. 2281–6.

force participation rates, and it included females. Significant technical and conceptual drawbacks remained, however.

1. The subcommittee's index included low earners, but made no effort to exclude those with current employment problems but more than adequate annual income. All workers paid less than $80 a week on a full-time basis, whether they were family heads and whether they had other sources of income, were included. If the subemployment index is to be a true measure of need, it makes a difference whether the low earner is a teenager in an affluent family, an unrelated individual, or the head of a large family. More than two-fifths of the unemployed in the poverty area sample, 35 percent of those working part-time for economic reasons, and 41 percent of the discouraged workers were wives and other relatives. Their "need" in some cases is questionable.[39]

2. The subcommittee's subemployment index was based on the labor market status of poverty area residents in the survey week. Measuring the rate of unemployment at a point in time misses many who combine low wages, recurrent unemployment, and stretches of nonparticipation in the work force. In the poverty areas, more than two-fifths of all persons with work experience were employed only part-year, and roughly half of these were unemployed at least once—twice the proportion recorded as unemployed in the survey week.[40] More than $80 a week is needed to provide a poverty level income if any substantial period is spent looking for work or outside the labor force. Either a work experience or minimum family income measure would be required to capture all those affected by both low wages and intermittent employment, i.e., those trapped in the secondary labor market.

3. The subcommittee's subemployment measure applied only to central city ghetto areas. Although much more inclusive than the 1967 data base, the Census Employment Survey still covered areas accounting for less than 6 percent of the nation's civilian noninstitutional population age 16 years and over. With no national baseline, it was impossible to tell whether the 30 percent rate of subemployment in the ghettos was substantially worse than else-

[39]U.S. Department of Commerce, Bureau of the Census, *Employment Profiles of Selected Low-Income Areas*, pp. 13, 19, 64.

[40]*Ibid.*, pp. 88, 94.

where—in which case the subemployment measure might only be worthwhile in dealing with central city populations—or whether subemployment was a pervasive phenomenon requiring national statistics to supplement other labor market measures in order to get a balanced perspective on employment and earnings problems.

To correct the first two shortcomings, an alternative subemployment index was derived and applied by Herman P. Miller, using the same Census Employment Survey data.[41] Like the subcommittee index, the revised measure included the unemployed, discouraged, involuntary part-time, and low-paid workers, but the categories were more rigorously defined. Persons 16 to 21 years of age who were primarily students, as well as persons age 65 years and over, were excluded on the assumption that they had less severe needs and were often marginally committed to the labor force. Only family heads and unrelated individuals were included in the low-paid groups, and they had to be earning less than $1.60 per hour or be working full-time but not earning enough to lift their households above the poverty line. This definition improved upon the subcommittee's approach by removing some of the groups whose need might be questioned and restricting the low earning category to primary breadwinners. Beyond this, however, the revised measure took another important step: it excluded all persons in families with above average incomes, thus yielding a more accurate indicator of need.

Applying this subemployment concept to the Census Employment Survey areas in the nation's 12 largest cities, 19.4 percent of the labor force was subemployed in 1970—a rate two-thirds of the subcommittee's index for the 60 areas. The exclusion of family members with above average incomes reduced the total of subemployed from 22.3 percent and the other definitional differences accounted for the rest.

This revised index had some drawbacks, however. For one thing, it did not come to grips with the problem of intermittent employment compounding low wages. Because a worker is currently employed full-time does not mean that he will work full-year.

[41]Herman P. Miller, "Subemployment in Poverty Areas of Large U.S. Cities," *Monthly Labor Review*, October 1973, pp. 10–17.

29

Another problem was that few unrelated individuals were screened out by the above average income test, which was based on the mean family income of the area. In the sampled poverty areas, this amounted to $11,000, or more than double the average for unrelated individuals. While their earnings could not be supplemented by the wages of other family members, they could be raised by other sources of income or they could be adequate (although less than the mean for families) despite the problems these persons experienced in the survey week.

The major drawback of the index, however, was that it was derived only for poverty areas in the 12 largest standard metropolitan statistical areas. These areas contained only three-fourths as many persons 16 years of age and over as the total CES sample used by the subcommittee, or less than 4 percent of the nation's adult population.

These various questions do not undermine the usefulness or the implications of the resurrected subemployment measures. Whatever technical and conceptual questions can be raised, the indices substantiated the fact that, at least in ghetto areas, the unemployment statistics counted only a minority of those who were failing in or being failed by the labor market.

# 2

## An Index of Employment and Earnings Inadequacy

Labor market measures are clearly not immutable, but rather a set of conventions useful only to the extent that they describe existing conditions, organize and quantify these in light of perceived theory, and generate information needed in addressing policy issues. The labor force statistics which emerged as an important monthly series at the end of the Great Depression were reexamined by the Gordon committee, subjected to continued scrutiny by a number of congressional groups and the federal agencies that produce and use the data, and analyzed intensively by academicians. In the process, the measures underwent several revisions, a variety of supplementary statistics were initiated, and increasing detail was provided.

More than three decades of sustained technical improvement of the Current Population Survey did much to improve the quality of the data, but the underlying concepts of measuring labor market deficiencies remained relatively unchanged. By the 1970s, labor market developments and changing policy and theoretical interpretations have increased the need to supplement the Current Population Survey with a new statistical measure that considers earnings as well as gainful employment. The 1970 recession, like those in the past, generated arguments over whether the unemployment rate overstated or understated the severity of conditions. But there were more deep-rooted considerations. The increase in the number of working wives, the rise in discretionary income and assets, and the growth of income maintenance programs reduced the correlation between unemployment and stark necessity. Labor statistics and public policy had focused on the unemployed, to the neglect of employed working poor who in many cases have even more serious difficulties. The subemployment indices were a step in the right direction, but they were not developed to the stage where they could serve as widely applicable social indicators.

## The Criteria

What is called for, then, is an additional index which will supplement the unemployment rate, by pulling together a range of separate labor market statistics and by building on previous subemployment concepts in order to measure the number of persons who experience difficulties in securing gainful employment at an adequate wage. Based on the preceding discussion, this new index will have to meet several criteria.

1. *Minimum standards of earnings adequacy based on family size and number of dependents are required. Whether or not it is a "failing" of the labor market that low wages cannot support large families, earnings adequacy must be measured relative to income needs.*

2. *The index must take account of the fact that low wages are frequently combined with intermittent employment. This requires data showing income flow for a longer period than a particular survey week.*

3. *Maximum income standards are also required to exclude individuals whose difficulties in the labor market do not jeopardize a socially accepted adequate standard of living.*

4. *In treating the family as a viable economic unit, the employment problems of secondary earners in families with adequate income should not be counted. Conversely, those whose income is critical in reaching a level below this standard should be included even if they are currently employed.*

5. *The problems of individuals who are outside the labor force or are employed part-time because jobs are unavailable must be considered, excluding those having little need for or commitment to work.*

6. *The index must be applicable for the total population. It must have meaning and be derived for different age, sex, race, and family status groups.*

Although normative elements cannot be eliminated, it is essential that the concepts be clearly defined and broadly understood. The Gordon committee's standards are applicable to the proposed index, i.e., it must be objectively measurable, operationally feasible, consistent with the "common" understanding of the concepts involved, and not so inclusive as to yield data which are difficult to interpret.[1]

In brief, the new index should be based upon an upper and lower bounded adequacy measure, weeding out those in the labor force who are too well off to be considered in need even if they experience employment problems, as well as pulling in those with "hidden" difficulties and frequently ignored needs. The goal is to develop a reasonably workable and broadly acceptable concept which, like the unemployment rate, can be refined and adjusted over the years. The Employment and Earnings Inadequacy (EEI) index is proposed as such a measure.

## Who Is Counted?

The EEI is derived by a three-step process: First, the "subemployed" are counted using a definition which seeks to overcome some of the shortcomings of previous indices. Second, all those subemployed in households with more than "adequate" incomes are excluded. Third, the total is divided by the number of labor force participants and discouraged workers to derive a single index.

Subemployment, as defined by EEI, is composed of the following:

---

[1]President's Committee to Appraise Employment and Unemployment Statistics, *Measuring Employment and Unemployment* (Washington: Government Printing Office, 1962), p. 43.

1. unemployed individuals who are willing, able and currently available for work, and who have taken definite steps in the last month to find a job;

2. discouraged workers who want jobs but are not looking because they think no work is available, lack the necessary experience or schooling, are too young or too old, or have other personal handicaps making them unattractive to employers;

3. currently employed family heads and unrelated individuals whose earnings in the previous 12 months were inadequate to lift their households above the poverty threshold;

4. other currently employed household heads earning less than a poverty income during the preceding year because of intermittent employment, less than full-time work and/or low wages; and,

5. workers employed part-time during the survey week, not included in the previous category, who want full-time jobs but cannot find them, have been laid off during the survey week, or have some other economic impediment requiring part-time employment.

Excluded from the subemployment definition and all of its categories are persons 16 to 21 years of age whose major activity is school attendance, and all those 65 years of age and over. These are arbitrary exclusions. The purpose is to remove groups whose attachment to the labor force is tenuous. Full-time students are usually working in or seeking only part-time jobs, and school dictates work patterns. Their standard and style of living is frequently different than for nonstudents and income "needs" are not easily defined. For instance, the college enrollee spending most of his or her time in college-related activities, normally financed out of comprehensive fees paid by parents, may be able to get along on a very low wage.

The exclusion of persons 65 years of age and over is based on the facts that public pensions now are nearly universal and private pensions widespread so that the labor force attachments of older individuals have become tenuous. Roughly 44 percent of all employed persons 65 years of age and over are part-time workers, many of whom receive social security and are discouraged by high marginal taxes from accepting full-time jobs. A large percentage of older full-time workers are also self-employed and can regulate the extent of work as they phase into retirement.

Despite these exclusions, the subemployed still include persons who may have employment problems but whose past earnings suggest that their economic needs do not constitute a severe personal or social problem. Many of the unemployed, discouraged, and involuntary part-time workers are wives or other family members, and although they may have problems related to work, the household head may be doing quite well. In addition, some of the family heads in these categories and some with low earnings may also be cushioned by the income of working wives or income other than earnings. In order to screen out the cases in which subemployment problems do not result in economic deprivation, upper income adequacy tests are applied to the household income for the year preceding the survey. All persons in households with above average income are not counted in the EEI total. Separate averages are used for residents of metropolitan and nonmetropolitan areas, and for families and unrelated individuals.

The EEI index is calculated as a ratio of the subemployed with below average incomes to the number of persons in the labor force, defined to include discouraged workers. The index indicates the proportion of people working, seeking work, or discouraged from seeking work who are unable to provide a minimum income and are also not fortunate enough to have other working family members or other sources of income which ameliorate the consequences of their own labor market problems.

## Derivation

The EEI index was developed so that it could be calculated from data collected each March in the extended household Current Population Survey (CPS). The derivation process described below is used to calculate separate EEI indices for sex, race, area of residence, and family status groups for 1968 through 1972.

There were 143 million persons 16 years of age and over in the civilian noninstitutional population in March 1972 (Table 1). Of these, 85.4 million were in the labor force and 0.7 million were discouraged nonstudents under age 65 years who wanted to work but thought no jobs were available. The adjusted labor force, for the purpose of the EEI calculations, is the sum of the two—86.1 million.

**Table 1. Derivation of Employment and Earnings Inadequacy Index for March 1972**

|  | Current Population Survey | Sub-employed | Persons in Households with Above Average Income | Employment and Earnings Inadequacy |
|---|---|---|---|---|
|  |  | *thousands* |  |  |
| Total population 16 years of age and over | 143,131 | — | — | — |
| Current population survey labor force | 85,398 | 85,398 | — | — |
| Current population survey discouraged workers | +830 | — | — | — |
| Less students 16 to 21 years of age and persons 65 years of age and over | −106 | — | — | — |
| Net discouraged workers | 724 | 724 | — | — |
| Adjusted labor force | — | 86,122 | — | 86,122 |
| (1) Unemployed | 5,215 | — | — | — |
| Less persons 65 years of age | −102 | — | — | — |
| Less students 16 to 21 years of age | −878 | — | — | — |

| | | | | |
|---|---|---|---|---|
| (3) Fully employed household heads earning less than poverty-level income | | | | |
| Family heads | 2,092 | — | — | — |
| Unrelated individuals | +243 | — | — | — |
| *Low-paid fully-employed heads* | 2,335 | 2,335 | -257 | 2,078 |
| (4) Partially employed household heads earning less than poverty level income | | | | |
| Family heads | 2,653 | — | — | — |
| Unrelated individuals | +1,029 | — | — | — |
| *Other low-earning heads* | 3,682 | 3,682 | -204 | 3,478 |
| (5) Employed part-time involuntarily | 2,312 | — | — | — |
| Less number included in above categories | -418 | — | — | — |
| *Involuntary part-time workers components* | 1,894 | 1,894 | -781 | 1,113 |
| Total subemployed and with inadequate employment and earnings | — | 12,870 | -2,298 | 9,942 |
| Subemployed and inadequately employed as percent of adjusted labor force | — | 14.9% | — | 11.5% |

The first step in estimating the percent of these actual or potential workers having inadequate employment and earnings is to derive the subemployment total and index.

1. The CPS counted 5.2 million unemployed workers in March 1972, but 0.1 million were individuals age 65 years and over and 0.9 million were 16- to 21-year-olds whose main activity was school, leaving 4.2 million unemployed included among the subemployed.

2. There were, as indicated, an additional 0.7 million nonstudent and nonelderly discouraged workers.

3. All currently employed family heads and unrelated individuals whose full-year, full-time, annual earnings during the previous year were inadequate to raise their families above the poverty threshold are included. The 1971 standard for unrelated individuals was $2,100 in nonfarm areas and $1,800 in farm areas. There were 0.2 million who were fully employed but earned less than these amounts. For families, the 1971 nonfarm thresholds were $2,725 for a two-person unit, $4,200 for one with four members, and $6,200 for one with seven members. There were 2.1 million family heads in 1971 who earned less than the relevant thresholds in the preceding year, though their families did not necessarily remain in poverty.

4. In the same manner, the previous year's earnings of employed family heads and unrelated individuals who worked less than full-time, full-year are compared with the poverty thresholds. There were 2.7 million family heads and 1.0 million unrelated individuals falling below the standard as a result of both intermittent employment and low wages.

5. In March 1972, 2.3 million persons 16 years of age and over worked part-time involuntarily for economic reasons. Excluding students and aged persons who are not included in the subemployment total, and household heads who in the last year earned less than poverty-level wages yielded 1.9 million, composed chiefly of wives and other relatives.

Adding these five components, there were 12.8 million subemployed in March 1972 out of the 86.1 million in the EEI-defined labor force. The subemployment rate was thus 14.9 percent.

To determine the number of subemployed who also have inadequate earnings, those in households with above average incomes for metropolitan or nonmetropolitan families or unrelated individuals must be subtracted. The March 1972 thresholds were $12,480 for families in SMSAs and $9,732 for those in nonmetropolitan areas. The comparable figures for unrelated individuals were $5,186 and $3,505, respectively. A third of the unemployed were in households with incomes above these averages, as were a fourth of discouraged workers, a tenth of low-paid fully employed household heads, 6 percent of other low-earning heads, and two-fifths of involuntary part-time workers. These differential reductions result because part-time, unemployed, and discouraged workers include secondary earners while, by definition, the low-wage categories do not. Overall, 2.9 of the 12.8 million subemployed in 1972 are excluded by the upper income screen. To calculate the EEI index, the reduced subemployed total, 9.9 million, is divided by the adjusted labor force, 86.1 million. This yields an index of 11.5 percent, as compared with the 14.9 percent subemployment rate.

## Technical and Conceptual Problems

There are a number of technical and conceptual difficulties with this proposed EEI index. Some of these can be corrected through further refinements using information available from the CPS; others require either additional data or a substantially revised definition of inadequacy.

*One issue is the exclusion of persons 65 years of age and over, and of students 16 to 21 years of age.* The argument is that most individuals in these groups have marginal attachments to the labor force since their income needs are normally met from other sources; other activities claim much of their time. Their employment difficulties are therefore mitigated and bear limited personal or social consequences, although exceptions may be considered critical. There is obviously no justification for excluding older workers who are not eligible for Social Security, who do not want to retire, or who have families to support. In 1971, there were an average of 109,000 unemployed persons 65 years of age and over, another 100,000 not in the labor force because they thought that jobs were not available for them, and roughly the same number employed part-time for economic reasons. There were also 91,000 who worked full-time, full-year, but still lived in poverty. About half a million thus might be added to the subemployed if all persons 65 years of age and over were included, increasing the inadequacy total by a twentieth. However, the case for inclusion is far from persuasive. Many have income from assets or are supported by families; most receive income transfers. In 1967, the last year for which detailed data are available, two-thirds of the married couples with a head 65 years of age or over reporting wage and salary income also received a public and/or private pension, as did nearly four-fifths of nonmarried earners.[2] Until some more refined standard can be formulated to include those with needs who experience difficulties in finding employment, and to exclude those with apparent difficulties but not very severe needs, it is a reasonable judgment to screen out those with real problems rather than including much larger numbers with questionable needs.

The exclusion of students 16 to 21 years of age also leaves out some persons with legitimate needs. Some 750,000 full-time male students were married in October 1971. Presumably, most of these had responsibilities as breadwinners. Also, earnings of students living with or helping to support their low-income families might be no less important than the earnings of other family members. There are, however, many more full-time students who would be questionably *in*cluded than there are those who are questionably *ex*cluded. The EEI methodology is probably appropriate in lieu of more refined determinations.

*A second issue is the choice of adequacy standards.* The lower thresholds for minimum earnings were based on the poverty levels because this concept is widely accepted and applied in the CPS. There are numerous alternatives, however. The near-poverty standard, i.e., 125 percent of the poverty threshold, could have been used. Alternatively, estimates of minimum living costs for

---

[2]Lenore Bixby, "Income of People Aged 65 and Older: Overview From 1968 Survey of the Aged," *Social Security Bulletin*, April 1970, pp. 3–25.

low income families—for instance, $7,183 for a family of four according to a Bureau of Labor Statistics calculation for New York City in 1971—could have been applied yielding a much more inclusive measure of inadequacy. The staff of the Senate Subcommittee on Employment, Manpower and Poverty used two different minimum standards in calculating its subemployment index: first, poverty level earnings or $80 a week; and, second, a level estimated to provide the low-income BLS living standard, or $140 weekly. The latter yielded a subemployment rate twice as high.[3]

The adequacy standard is arbitrary, but the choice of poverty thresholds is the most reasonable in terms of the Gordon committee's criteria, that an index be objective, operationally feasible, consistent with common understanding, and not overly inclusive.

1. The poverty thresholds or multiples thereof are adjusted only for cost-of-living changes and therefore allow for measurement of progress over time, while the BLS minimum budget estimates rise with real income.

2. The poverty thresholds are more operationally feasible since they are calculated for families of different sizes and for nonfarm areas, while the BLS figures are currently limited to a selected number of metropolitan areas.

3. The poverty thresholds, as opposed to the 125-percent-of-poverty figures, are probably more consistent with common usage and the accepted interpretation of need. To have operational significance, the index must focus on the population that faces special difficulties competing in the labor market; the broader its base, the less its value as a needs indicator.

The upper bounds for excluding families and individuals with more than "adequate" income are also arbitrary. There are wide variations between different metropolitan and nonmetropolitan areas, and regional breakdowns might change the picture. There is also a significant differential between the average income and needs of families of different sizes. These are taken into account in the poverty thresholds but not in the average income data used

[3]U.S. Congress, Senate Subcommittee on Employment, Manpower and Poverty, "The Subemployment: 1970 Rates and Wirtz Memorandums," in *Comprehensive Manpower Reform*, 1972, Part 5, 92nd cong., 2nd sess. (Washington: Government Printing Office, April 1972), pp. 2276–80.

for upper screens. Conceivably, upper adequacy bounds could be adjusted according to the number of family members. Measures other than mean income could also be adopted. The medians for families and unrelated individuals are one obvious alternative and might be considered preferrable, but were not available for this study. In 1971, when the median incomes for families and unrelated individuals were 88 and 68 percent, respectively, of the means, their use would have resulted in more persons being excluded, and a lower subemployment index. In 1972, the median screen would leave 9.2 rather than 9.9 million persons with inadequate employment and earnings, reducing the EEI from 11.5 to 10.6 percent.

*A third issue is the mixing of time frames in the EEI.* The use of earnings in the previous year as opposed to earnings during the survey week is necessitated by the limitations of the CPS sample. The former is probably preferrable since many workers with intermittent employment patterns and frequent entry and reentry into the labor market may end up with inadequate earnings though employed at a barely adequate wage in the survey week. However, there are some undesirable consequences of using last year's experience as a proxy for current status. If a person's family or employment status changed through marriage, divorce, monetary windfalls, or temporary setbacks, misleading data might be recorded. An individual might also have entered or reentered the labor force at sometime in the last year, making his recorded yearly earnings below the poverty threshold although at a weekly or monthly rate they would be far above it. Revisions might be desirable in the "other low-earning heads" category to weed out new labor force entrants, and other adjustments could be made if additional questions were asked in the CPS about status changes. It is assumed, however, that at the level of accuracy for which the EEI index aspires, these factors will either cancel each other or be relatively constant from year to year.

It might also be argued that an adequate income in the preceding year does not mitigate the impact of current unemployment, since all of the money may have been spent, leaving no savings. And quite clearly, the level of the past year's income does not shed any light on whether unemployment compensation or other transfer payments are currently available to alleviate needs and perhaps to delay the return to work for the unemployed. If *weekly* income and earning data were gathered in the Current Population Survey questionnaire, adjustments could be made.

*A related issue is the inclusion of currently unemployed persons, regardless of their prior work experience.* An alternative approach used in the 1968 *Manpower Report of the President* was to base the subemployment measure on the unemployment experience over the last year rather than on current status. This system would seem more appropriate, or at least consistent with the earnings experience components of the EEI index, but it does have some disadvantages. Only those with 15 or more weeks of unemployment in the previous year were included in the 1968 measure. This left out many workers with shorter unemployment spells which gave them net earnings below the poverty threshold. But a lower standard, for instance four weeks, would include many other volatile labor force participants whose unemployment was related to frequent entrance and exit from the job market. The aim is to include only those whose intermittent work leads to low earnings and a low standard of living. To accomplish this, the EEI uses a minimum earnings standard to assess the impact of intermittency, including in the measure those who may be periodically discouraged or otherwise forced to leave the labor force, even though they may not be unemployed.

But the inclusion of all the currently unemployed (minus 16- to 21-year-old students, persons 65 years of age and over, and those in households with above average incomes) rather than just those who have a pattern of unemployment and/or low wages in the previous year is a questionable decision. The reason for this broader measure is that there is a wide range of "need" between the mean family income and the poverty level income. Some weighting might be justified so that the currently unemployed individual who earned, say, $8,000 in the previous year but during the current year earned only $6,000 because of unemployment is not given as much weight in computing the inadequacy index as the full-time, full-year worker earning less than a poverty level wage. But in the absence of refined standards or data on currently available assets and alternative sources of support, it must be assumed that those who are out of work and have their less-than-average income reduced by forced idleness are objects of social concern. The EEI does not assert that all persons counted are equally needy, but rather that by accepted societal standards, these people are facing problems in the labor market. Critics may argue that the index mixes "apples and oranges" since those currently unemployed may not be the same as those with low earnings in the past year. But such diversity has been accepted in the unemployment rate, which includes recent entrants as well as displaced skilled workers unemployed for 15 weeks or more as well as family heads and student part-time jobseekers. No index can avoid such difficulties, especially when it tries to capture the multi-dimensioned aspects of employment problems and economic need.

While the mixing of employment and earning time frames in the EEI index may be warranted, there are significant ramifications. The number of unemployed changes dramatically from month to month, but the number of households or individuals with low earnings reacts more slowly and less extensively to the business cycle. The EEI is not as seasonally or cyclically sensitive a measure as the unemployment rate. Its real purpose is to reflect changes in the labor market and in the welfare of labor force participants over the longer run rather than week-to-week or month-to-month. For this purpose, annual, or at most, quarterly, calculations are probably sufficient, although much more geographic detail would be needed to use the EEI for policy determination.

*A fifth issue is that only household heads with low earnings are included in the EEI.* The spouse or other relative of a low-earning family head might be working and also earning very little; their combined income is likely to be below the upper adequacy bound and perhaps even the minimum poverty threshold. An extra dollar from either one is equally meaningful and it might be argued that the secondary worker in this case should be included in the EEI index. A more precise inadequacy measure could be designed to include low-earning secondary workers in low-income families.

*Sixth, questions might be raised about the adequacy of the Bureau of Labor Statistics's discouraged worker definition.* The

Senate Subcommittee on Employment, Manpower, and Poverty counted as subemployed all nonparticipants wanting a job and giving the unavailability of work as a reason. On the other hand, the BLS excludes anyone who has home or school responsibilities, ill health, or other reasons for not working even if they also indicate that they are discouraged. The total would have been half again as high if everyone indicating discouragement were counted, whatever their other activities. Creators of the EEI index opted for consistency rather than trying to rewrite the definition.

*Seventh, the iterative process used in calculating the subemployment total affects the level of its components.* For instance, some of the current involuntary part-time workers were subject to unemployment and involuntary part-time work in the past, and appear in the other low earnings group. If part-time workers were counted first, the number included in the low earnings group would have been smaller, although the subemployment and EEI totals would not be affected.

*Finally, the labor force plus discouraged worker totals were used as the denominator in calculating the EEI index.* It might have been appropriate to subtract 16- to 21-year-old students and persons 65 years of age and over from the labor force to make the denominator consistent with the components of the numerator. This would have resulted in a slightly higher index, and might have been justified if there were significant annual changes in the student and elderly portions of the labor force. But since these groups are excluded on the assumption that they are not in need, just as persons in above average income families are excluded, they probably should continue to be counted in the labor force.

## A Reasonable Measure

Despite the conceptual and technical difficulties, the EEI index improves upon earlier attempts to measure the adequacy of employment and earnings in several ways.

1. The EEI provides a minimum earnings measure which includes those who are employed but have earnings problems or are in seasonal or high turnover jobs. Since it focuses on annual earnings, the index avoids the questionable projection of weekly

earnings into a full-year income and includes those individuals with a greater probability of intermittent employment and low earnings.

2. The EEI screens out those whose labor market problems are not likely to generate income problems. The use of the family income measure takes some account of earnings by secondary workers and of other sources of income. This alleviates many of the reservations raised about the inclusiveness of earlier subemployment measures.

3. The EEI attempts to focus on "real" labor market problems by including only household heads among the low earnings components and excluding marginal job searchers—16- to 21-year-old students and individuals 65 years of age and over.

4. On the other hand, the EEI index rejects the current arbitrary counting of part-time workers who want full-time jobs as being "employed" and the exclusion of the discouraged workers from the labor force.

5. The EEI index generally meets the Gordon committee criteria for an effective measure. Though discouragement and involuntary part-time employment must be determined from subjective self-assessments, the data on these components have been gathered for some time, and there is every evidence that these subjective perceptions have a predictable correlation with objective reality. The EEI concept is not as "clean" or objective as the unemployment rate because it relies upon some arbitrary parameters, but its components are measurable with a fair degree of accuracy.

Certainly, the EEI index is practicable. It was structured so that it could be derived from information already gathered in the extended household survey each March. Its calculation and publication on a permanent annual basis could be achieved at a small cost (less than a tenth of a percent of current BLS annual budget, based on the cost of the present calculations). Other information might be needed to refine the measure, but the point is that the EEI index as outlined can be derived effectively without much additional gathering of data.

The EEI concepts have been kept as simple as possible and have been based on the most commonly accepted notions. As an example, the poverty threshold figures were used for the lower adequacy standards on the assumption that these were the most easily understandable.

Finally, the assumptions used in defining the EEI index were restrictive. Few would question the needs of those counted as having inadequate employment and earnings. The exclusion of students and older workers, the inclusion of only household heads among low-earners, and the screening out of persons with higher incomes, yields an index concentrated on persons with labor market problems.

In summary, then, the proposed EEI index represents a reasonable measurement, although technical problems remain which require further refinement. Because it is a composite, overlaying concepts of income and employment, the issues involved are complex and the achievement of a measure as technically pure as the unemployment rate is not promising. The value of the index does not depend on its absolute precision, but rather on its effectiveness in describing reality and in addressing critical policy problems. Whether or not it is a "good" index depends on whether it sheds light on labor market conditions and provides needed information for policymakers. This can only be determined by calculating the EEI, analyzing the cross-sectional and longitudinal data, and applying the resulting information to policy issues.

# 3

## The EEI Index for March 1972

### An Overview

Inadequate employment and earnings are widespread. In March 1972, when 5.2 million persons 16 years of age and over were out of work, 9.9 million were counted by the EEI (table 2). While the unemployment rate was 6.1 percent, the EEI Index stood at 11.5 percent. The index suggests that one in nine workers faced labor market problems which had serious consequences for their well-being. Alternative definitions of the index would have yielded different results, but the following conclusions emerge from the derivation of the EEI which in all likelihood would prevail under reasonable alternative formulations.

1. *Low earnings are more frequently a source of deprivation than unemployment.* In March 1972, the unemployed accounted for only 27.5 percent of the EEI total. Even if discouraged and involuntarily part-time workers are added on the assumption that they, too, have problems finding employment, the total of the three groups accounted for less than half of the index.

2. *Many of the unemployed do not have severe needs.* Only 2.7 million of the 5.2 million unemployed in March 1972 had inadequate employment and earnings. The remainder were 16- to 21-year-old students, persons 65 years of age and over, or members of households with above average incomes.

Table 2. Components of the EEI Index, March 1972

|  | (thousands) | Percent of EEI | Mean Household Income | Percent Households in Poverty |
|---|---|---|---|---|
| In adjusted labor force | 86,122 | — | $11,528 | 6.9% |
| With inadequate employment and earnings | 9,942 | 100.0% | 4,780 | 42.6 |
| Unemployed | 2,731 | 27.5 | 6,070 | 26.3 |
| Discouraged workers | 542 | 5.5 | 4,743 | 43.4 |
| Low paid fully employed heads | 2,078 | 20.9 | 4,245 | 58.3 |
| Other low earning heads | 3,478 | 35.0 | 3,712 | 55.5 |
| Employed part-time involuntarily | 1,113 | 11.2 | 6,642 | 12.5 |
| EEI Index | 11.5% | — | — | — |

3. *The compounding of low wages and intermittent employment is a significant problem.* Family heads who worked less than full-time, full-year, and earned below a poverty income accounted for 35 percent of the EEI total in March 1972. The heads had extremely low average incomes and their needs were clearly critical.

4. *Poverty is widespread among persons included in the EEI.* The average annual household income of persons with inadequate employment and earnings in March 1972 was only $4,780—two-fifths the average family income of all labor force participants. The incidence of poverty was more than six times greater in the EEI universe than in the labor force overall.

## The Relationship Between Employment and Income Problems

A major difference between the EEI and earlier subemployment formulations is the exclusion of individuals in households with above average income. This is an important distinction, since employment problems do not always result in economic distress. Of the 12.9 million persons counted by the EEI definitions as subemployed in March 1972, 23 percent were in households with above average incomes in the previous year (table 3). A substantial

**Table 3. Impact of Screening Out Members of Households With Above Average Income, March 1972**

| Category | Subemployed | Persons with Inadequate Employment and Earnings | Percentage Decline as Result of Income Screen | Mean Annual Household Income | | |
|---|---|---|---|---|---|---|
| | | | | Subemployed | Persons with Inadequate Employment and Earnings | Percentage Decline as a Result of Above Average Income Screen |
| | *(thousands)* | *(thousands)* | | | | |
| TOTAL | 12,869 | 9,942 | 22.7% | $ 7,340 | $4,780 | 34.9% |
| Family heads | 6,834 | 5,839 | 14.6 | 6,695 | 5,055 | 24.5 |
| Wives | 1,921 | 1,217 | 36.6 | 10,227 | 7,104 | 30.5 |
| Other relatives | 2,171 | 1,200 | 44.7 | 12,627 | 6,615 | 47.6 |
| Unrelated individuals | 1,942 | 1,686 | 13.2 | 2,483 | 1,671 | 32.7 |
| Males | 7,709 | 5,948 | 22.8 | 7,550 | 4,963 | 34.3 |
| Females | 5,160 | 3,994 | 22.6 | 7,059 | 4,595 | 34.9 |
| Whites | 10,177 | 7,614 | 25.2 | 7,729 | 4,859 | 37.1 |
| Blacks | 2,500 | 2,185 | 12.6 | 5,626 | 4,501 | 20.0 |
| Metropolitan residents | 8,155 | 6,376 | 21.8 | 7,807 | 5,108 | 34.6 |
| Nonmetropolitan residents | 4,714 | 3,566 | 24.4 | 6,524 | 4,186 | 35.8 |
| Unemployed | 4,235 | 2,731 | 35.5 | 9,834 | 6,070 | 38.3 |
| Discouraged workers | 724 | 542 | 25.1 | 7,629 | 4,743 | 37.8 |
| Low-paid, fully-employed heads | 2,335 | 2,078 | 11.0 | 5,452 | 4,245 | 22.1 |
| Other low-earning heads | 3,682 | 3,478 | 5.5 | 4,320 | 3,712 | 14.1 |
| Involuntary part-time employment | 1,894 | 1,113 | 41.2 | 10,656 | 6,642 | 37.7 |

proportion of the unemployed, discouraged, and involuntary part-time subemployed workers were excluded from the EEI index. On the other hand, supplementary earnings of secondary workers and income from other sources rarely proved adequate to lift the households headed by low-paid workers above the average family income.

A third of the individuals who were screened out were family heads, a fourth were wives, a third other relatives, and the remainder were unrelated individuals. Stated another way, 37 percent of all subemployed wives and 45 percent of other relatives were excluded from the EEI on the assumption that they were secondary earners whose wages contributed to more than adequate family incomes. The reasons for the exclusion of only 13 percent of unrelated individuals are not as apparent. The adequacy standard for unrelated individuals might not have been restrictive enough. If median rather than mean income had been used as upper adequacy bound, the proportion excluded would have risen to 23 percent because of the lower median-to-mean income ratio of unrelated individuals, although their share of the EEI index would have been only slightly lower. Only a small proportion of unrelated individuals were screened by either approach, since families can have two or more earners raising income above the upper bound, while unrelated individuals must rely on other sources of income.

It is not surprising to find that the white subemployed were twice as likely to have above-average incomes. Since their household income average was a fourth higher than that of blacks, they were more frequently excluded from the needs index.

The fact that males and females have roughly the same probability of exclusion must be interpreted carefully. By definition, wives are not counted in the low earnings groups. In the other three subemployment categories, however, one might expect that women would be more frequently excluded by the above average income test because of their presumed secondary earning status. This was not the case. The upper income limit reduced the number of unemployed, discouraged, and involuntary part-time male workers by 39 percent, but female workers by only 33 percent. The claim is often made that discouragement or unemployment of females is not important, since they are "peripheral" workers. However, a larger share of males than females included in these categories were in households with above average incomes which were attributable to other family earners or sources of income.

To the extent that economic need can be measured in terms of household income in the preceding year, the screening process is vital to reduce the average income among the subemployed to a level which most people would agree is inadequate. The mean annual income of all subemployed households was $7,340— certainly not a level of dire necessity. For the unemployed, the mean was $9,834, and for persons working part-time involuntarily it was $10,656, suggesting the presence of many in these categories who were not being motivated by economic necessity. When the upper income screen was applied, the mean income of these two groups fell 38 percent. Overall, the average household income of persons with inadequate employment and earnings was $4,780, or 35 percent less than that of the subemployed. At the other end of the income spectrum, the average household income of the excluded unemployed, discouraged and part-time workers was over $16,000. Although a high level of previous income may not have guaranteed them a cushion against current adversity, most of the persons excluded were undoubtedly better off than the majority who remained in the EEI index.

### EEI As A Measure of Need

The EEI singles out those whose employment problems generate or compound income problems; 43 percent of those with inadequate employment and earnings lived in poverty and their mean household income was less than half the national average in 1972. There were differences, however. Wives and other relatives were generally in families with higher incomes than those of included family heads (table 4). Only 14 percent of unemployed, discouraged, and involuntary part-time working wives were in families which were poor, and their mean household income was $7,104. Males in the same three categories averaged only $4,481 in income, with 23 percent living in poverty. Working wives either supplement their families' incomes over the course of the year despite their problems or are drawn disproportionately from higher income units. It may also be true that in families in which the head

**Table 4.  Mean Household Income and Poverty Incidence Among Individuals With Inadequate Employment and Earnings, March 1972**

|  | *Annual Household Mean Income* | *Percent Poor* |
|---|---|---|
| TOTAL | $4,780 | 42.6% |
| Family heads | 5,055 | 42.9 |
| Wives | 7,104 | 14.1 |
| Other relatives | 6,615 | 28.5 |
| Unrelated individuals | 1,671 | 72.0 |
| Males | 4,963 | 42.2 |
| Females | 4,595 | 43.2 |
| Whites | 4,859 | 39.3 |
| Blacks | 4,501 | 53.4 |
| Metropolitan residents | 5,108 | 38.9 |
| Nonmetropolitan residents | 4,186 | 49.1 |
| Unemployed | 6,070 | 26.3 |
| Discouraged workers | 4,743 | 43.4 |
| Low-paid, fully-employed heads | 4,245 | 58.3 |
| Other low-earning heads | 3,712 | 55.5 |
| Involuntary part-time employment | 6,642 | 12.5 |

earns very little, the wives are likely to put out more effort finding jobs and consequently to be less frequently unemployed, discouraged, or employed part-time involuntarily.

The income and poverty incidence data should further dispel doubts about the stringency of the upper income screen for unrelated individuals. The mean income for this EEI category was only $1,671 and 72.0 percent were in poverty.

The mean household income of blacks with inadequate employment and earnings was 7 percent below that of whites (even though a higher percentage of whites were screened out by the upper income limits). Black male family heads included in the EEI had a higher mean income than white family heads, but the averages for wives, other relatives, and especially unrelated individuals were much lower. More than half of blacks with inadequate employment and earnings were classified as poor, compared with less than two-fifths of whites.

Income was higher and poverty less frequent in urban areas. The $5,108 average income for metropolitan households was 22 percent higher than for nonmetropolitan households. Nonmetropolitan residents in the EEI were worse off since only an eighth were unrelated individuals having lesser needs, compared with a sixth of the persons with inadequacy in metropolitan areas. In part, this difference reflects differentials in living costs. Although the poverty thresholds attempt to adjust for these differentials, half of nonmetropolitan residents with inadequate employment and earnings were classified as poor, compared with only 39 percent of those in SMSAs.

Despite the fact that a large percentage of persons are screened from the unemployed and involuntary part-time categories, those remaining in these categories are usually better off than others in the EEI. More than half of the households headed by discouraged and low-paid workers lived in poverty, compared with 26 percent of those unemployed and 13 percent of those employed part-time involuntarily. Among the unemployed, this still modest income in the previous year may offer little protection against current interruption of earnings. But it is less clear that part-time involuntary workers are in need. Those who have patterns of low earnings and are household heads are included in the "other low earning heads" category, while those who are counted in the involuntary part-time category, unlike the unemployed, have at least some current earnings. The involuntary part-time worker component of the EEI might therefore be eliminated as the index is refined in order to exclude those with doubtful hardship.

## The Incidence of Inadequacy

The incidence of inadequacy varies significantly among different groups. Some of the differences—those between blacks and whites and those between metropolitan and nonmetropolitan residents—reflect straightforwardly the diversity of their employment problems. Other differentials—those between the sexes and between persons with differing family status—may be in part definitional. More than a fourth of blacks (but less than a tenth of whites) have inadequate employment and earnings (table 5). The EEI index among residents of nonmetropolitan areas is three-

Table 5. Incidence of Inadequate Employment and Earnings and Its Components, March 1972

| Category | EEI Index | Percent of EEI-Defined Labor Force | | | | |
| --- | --- | --- | --- | --- | --- | --- |
| | | Unemployed | Discouraged | Low-paid Fully-employed Heads | Other Low-Paid Heads | Employed Part-Time Involuntarily |
| Family heads | 13.7 | 2.5 | 0.3 | 4.3 | 5.8 | .8 |
| Wives | 6.3 | 3.4 | 0.9 | — | — | 2.0 |
| Other relatives | 7.8 | 4.6 | 1.2 | — | — | 2.0 |
| Unrelated individuals | 19.0 | 3.6 | 0.4 | 2.7 | 11.3 | 1.0 |
| Males | 11.3 | 2.8 | 0.3 | 3.2 | 4.0 | 1.0 |
| Females | 11.9 | 3.7 | 1.1 | 1.2 | 4.1 | 1.8 |
| Whites | 10.0 | 2.7 | 0.4 | 2.1 | 3.6 | 1.2 |
| Blacks | 25.2 | 7.1 | 2.1 | 5.6 | 7.8 | 2.6 |
| Male  -whites | 9.9 | 2.5 | 0.2 | 2.7 | 3.7 | 0.9 |
|     blacks | 24.7 | 6.2 | 1.7 | 7.3 | 7.2 | 2.4 |
| Female-whites | 10.0 | 3.1 | 0.8 | .9 | 3.5 | 1.6 |
|     blacks | 25.8 | 8.2 | 2.6 | 3.5 | 8.6 | 2.9 |
| Metropolitan residents | 10.6 | 3.4 | 0.5 | 1.7 | 3.8 | 1.2 |
| Nonmetropolitan residents | 13.7 | 2.7 | 0.8 | 4.1 | 4.7 | 1.4 |
| Metropolitan   whites | 9.0 | 2.8 | 0.4 | 1.3 | 3.4 | 1.1 |
|     blacks | 22.9 | 7.6 | 1.7 | 4.5 | 6.7 | 2.3 |
| Nonmetropolitan   whites | 12.0 | 2.5 | 0.6 | 3.6 | 4.0 | 1.3 |
|     blacks | 32.4 | 5.3 | 3.4 | 9.0 | 11.3 | 3.4 |

tenths higher than among those in metropolitan areas. These differences result from the fact that blacks and nonmetropolitan residents of all characteristics tend to have more frequent employment and earnings problems. It should be noted, however, that females are only slightly more likely than males to be included in the EEI index, mainly because of the exclusion of wives from the low-paid groups. Including low-earning wives and then screening out those in families with above average income would have increased the rate of inclusion of women in the EEI. If this were done, however, it then would have been unclear whether the women's low earnings reflected failure in the labor market or frequent entrance and exit due to family responsibilities. The upper adequacy bound alone cannot distinguish between a low-paid family member working a few hours a year (with the head providing an income only slightly below average) and a wife who has the major breadwinning responsibility. To alleviate this confusion, the EEI was limited to persons whose needs could not be easily questioned, thus excluding low-earning wives. The result was the relatively lower EEI rates for females.

But the relative status of females is less favorable than the aggregate indices suggest. Statistics from March 1972 indicated that women were 32 percent more likely to be unemployed, 80 percent more likely to be employed part-time involuntarily for economic reasons, and 3.7 times more likely to be discouraged. While women were underrepresented in the low-paid group because of the exclusion of wives, female family heads participating in the labor force were more than twice as likely as male family heads to be full-time, full-year workers with earnings below the poverty threshold. Unrelated female participants also had a 25 percent higher chance of being in the fully-employed, low-earnings group than unrelated males.

## Race and Residence

The EEI and its components shed further light on black/white and metropolitan/nonmetropolitan differentials (table 6). Blacks have more frequent and severe labor problems than whites, with an EEI rate 2.5 times as high. One group with especially severe

**Table 6. Ratio of Black/White and Nonmetropolitan/Metropolitan EEIs and Components**

| Category | Ratio of EEI Indices | Relative Incidence | | | | |
|---|---|---|---|---|---|---|
| | | Unemployed | Discouraged | Low-Paid Fully-Employed Heads | Other Low-Paid Heads | Employed Part-Time Involuntarily |
| Black/White | 2.5 | 2.6 | 5.3 | 2.7 | 2.2 | 2.2 |
| Male | 2.5 | 2.5 | 8.5 | 2.7 | 1.9 | 2.7 |
| Family head | 2.7 | 2.0 | 5.0 | 3.4 | 2.5 | 2.1 |
| Other relative | 3.1 | 2.5 | 8.2 | — | — | 2.4 |
| Unrelated individual | 1.6 | 2.2 | 3.5 | 1.3 | 1.2 | 3.1 |
| Female | 2.6 | 2.6 | 3.3 | 3.9 | 2.5 | 1.8 |
| Family head | 1.5 | 2.1 | 1.4 | 2.0 | 1.4 | — |
| Wife | 2.1 | 2.1 | 2.0 | — | — | 2.0 |
| Other relative | 4.3 | 3.8 | 8.3 | — | — | 3.6 |
| Unrelated individual | 1.8 | 2.3 | 2.6 | 1.8 | 1.7 | 1.1 |
| Nonmetropolitan/Metropolitan | 1.3 | .8 | 1.6 | 2.4 | 1.2 | 1.2 |
| Black | 1.4 | .7 | 2.0 | 2.0 | 1.7 | 1.5 |
| Family head | 1.7 | .7 | .5 | 2.2 | 2.1 | .6 |
| Wife | .9 | .6 | — | — | — | 1.5 |
| Other relative | 1.2 | .7 | 2.6 | — | — | 1.3 |
| Unrelated individual | 1.6 | .5 | — | 2.3 | 1.7 | 1.9 |
| White | 1.3 | .9 | 1.5 | 2.8 | 1.2 | 1.2 |
| Family head | 1.6 | 1.0 | 1.8 | 2.9 | 1.3 | .4 |
| Wife | 1.1 | 1.3 | 1.9 | — | — | 1.4 |
| Other relative | 1.0 | .9 | .6 | — | — | 1.5 |
| Unrelated individuals | 1.3 | .5 | 4.4 | 1.9 | 1.4 | .5 |

problems is the black "other relative" category, apparently indicating the critical black youth unemployment. Black males in this category had a rate of inclusion in the EEI three times that of whites, and the inclusion of black females in the EEI was more than four times as high as for white females. The significance of this disturbing high level of inadequacy is compounded by the fact that the "other relative" group constitutes a much larger proportion of the black than the white labor force.

Based on the black/white ratios, it would appear that female family heads were relatively better off than other blacks, since their EEI was 1.5 times as high as for white female heads. But relative status may be misleading, since the EEI index for black women heading families was an alarming 55 percent in 1972. Any woman who is a family head is likely to have inadequate employment and earnings.

For unrelated individuals, the black/white comparisons also mask the extent of the problems. The 26 percent EEI index for male black unrelated individuals was only 1.6 times that for whites, while the 34 percent black female rate for unrelated individuals was only 1.8 times as high. It is of little comfort to the many unattached blacks with problems that white unrelated individuals also have severe difficulties.

Male family heads represent the largest category in the EEI index and their employment and earnings problems bear consequences for all family members. The index for black family heads was 2.7 times that for whites, and blacks were 3.4 times as likely to be full-time full-year workers earning less than a poverty level wage.

Area differences were also significant. The unemployment rate for nonmetropolitan residents was almost a fifth lower than for those living in metropolitan areas. However, the incidence of low earnings among the fully employed in nonmetropolitan areas was two and a half times as high, while the percentage in the other low-paid heads category was also a fourth higher. The farm/nonfarm poverty threshold differentials may be more stringent for metropolitan than nonmetropolitan residents. But the underlying fact is well documented that wage rates in nonmetropolitan areas are much lower than in SMSAs.

The data indicate that wives and other relatives were not much worse off in nonmetropolitan than in metropolitan areas, but this may be a spurious conclusion. These groups are not included in the low-paying categories, where nonmetropolitan workers face relatively greater problems.

Blacks outside the SMSAs were twice as likely—and whites 2.7 times as likely—as their counterparts in metropolitan areas to be full-time, full-year workers earning less than a poverty level wage. For black family heads, there was a 70 percent higher chance of having inadequate employment and earnings in nonmetropolitan areas; for unrelated individuals the chances were 60 percent higher. These ratios were only slightly higher than those for whites, but in absolute terms, the problems of blacks outside SMSAs were staggering. Nearly half of all black family heads, and 43 percent of unrelated individuals, were included in the 1972 EEI index.

### Shares of the Universe of Need

The distribution of the EEI by sex, race, residence, and family status also deserves scrutiny. Nearly three-fifths of the 9.9 million persons with inadequate employment and earnings in March 1972 were family heads (table 7). Since wives and other relatives were most frequently screened out by the EEI definition and the upper income test, they accounted for only a fourth of the total, while unrelated individuals added 17 percent. Family heads constituted a minority of the unemployed, discouraged, and involuntarily part-time workers, but they accounted for 89 percent of the full-time, full-year workers earning less than a poverty level wage, again reflecting the exclusion of wives and other relatives from the category. Because they were underrepresented in the low-earnings groups, females constituted only two-fifths of the total EEI, but comprised 46 percent of the unemployed, 70 percent of the discouraged, and 53 percent of those employed part-time involuntarily. Blacks counted for 22 percent of those with inadequate employment and earnings, but 34 percent of all discouraged workers. Nonmetropolitan residents represented only 26 percent of the unemployed, but 51 percent of low-paid, fully-employed heads and 36 percent of persons in the EEI.

**Table 7. Distribution of Inadequate Employment and Earnings by Category, March 1972**

| Category | EEI Total | Unemployed | Discouraged | Fully-Employed Low-Paid Heads | Other Low-Earning Heads | Employed Part-Time Involuntarily |
|---|---|---|---|---|---|---|
| Family heads | 59 | 39 | 26 | 89 | 71 | 30 |
| Male | (45) | (31) | ( 9) | (75) | (49) | (25) |
| Female | (14) | ( 8) | (17) | (14) | (22) | ( 5) |
| Wives | 12 | 24 | 33 | — | — | 35 |
| Other relatives | 12 | 26 | 35 | — | — | 27 |
| Unrelated relatives | 17 | 12 | 7 | 11 | 29 | 8 |
| Males | 60 | 54 | 30 | 80 | 61 | 47 |
| Females | 40 | 46 | 70 | 20 | 39 | 53 |
| Whites | 77 | 76 | 61 | 76 | 79 | 79 |
| Blacks | 22 | 22 | 34 | 23 | 20 | 20 |
| Male   Whites | 47 | 43 | 15 | 62 | 50 | 37 |
| Blacks | 12 | 11 | 15 | 17 | 10 | 10 |
| Female   Whites | 29 | 33 | 46 | 13 | 29 | 42 |
| Blacks | 10 | 12 | 19 | 7 | 10 | 11 |
| Metropolitan residents | 64 | 74 | 61 | 49 | 65 | 67 |
| Nonmetropolitan residents | 36 | 26 | 40 | 51 | 35 | 33 |

## Central City Inadequacy

To assess the significance of the earlier subemployment measures which focused on poverty areas in large central cities, the March 1972 EEI index and its components were derived for central cities. "Central cities" include the largest city in each SMSA as well as other cities with at least 250,000 inhabitants or a population one-third that of the largest city and a minimum of 25,000 persons. The 1970 Census Employment Survey covered poverty areas with adult populations of under 8 million, in which a fourth of families were poor. In contrast, the central cities contained 42.2 million adults in March 1972 with only 11 percent of the families counted in poverty. Yet, central city conditions were poorer than those in the remaining areas within the SMSAs. The central city EEI in March 1972 was 13.1 percent, compared with 8.6 percent in the suburbs (table 8). Although they represented only 45 percent of SMSA labor force participants, central city residents 16 years of age and over accounted for 55 percent of those with inadequate employment and earnings. On the other hand, it is important to note that inadequate income and employment are not just central city phenomena. The suburban rings contained 29 percent of all persons in the nation with inadequate employment and earnings. These 2.8 million persons had severe problems even if they were "underrepresented" in the suburban population.

There are very significant differences between inadequate employment and earnings in the central city and elsewhere. One dimension of this difference is the heavy concentration of blacks, nearly three-fifths of whom lived in central cities where they represented three-tenths of the adult population in 1972. Conversely, 17 percent of adult blacks were suburbanites, compared with two-fifths of all persons. It is not surprising, then, that while a third of those with inadequate employment and earnings in the central cities were black, only a tenth of those in like circumstances in the suburbs were black (table 9). Wherever they were located, blacks were in less favorable financial conditions than the whites. Suburban residence was associated with a somewhat lesser chance of failure, but it was no panacea. Suburban blacks had an EEI 2.4 times that of suburban whites—a ratio higher than in central cities.

**Table 8. Inadequate Employment and Earnings by Area of Residence, March 1972**

| | U.S. Total | Outside SMSA | SMSA | Central Cities | Suburban Ring |
|---|---|---|---|---|---|
| | | | *(thousands)* | | |
| Population 16 years of age and over | 143,131 | 44,309 | 98,821 | 42,212 | 56,609 |
| Labor force | 86,122 | 25,943 | 60,179 | 27,050 | 33,129 |
| Subemployment | 12,869 | 4,714 | 8,155 | 4,262 | 3,893 |
| Inadequate employment and earnings | 9,942 | 3,566 | 6,376 | 3,531 | 2,845 |
| Family heads | 5,839 | 2,327 | 3,512 | 1,887 | 1,625 |
| Wives | 1,217 | 426 | 791 | 384 | 407 |
| Other relatives | 1,200 | 383 | 817 | 441 | 376 |
| Unrelated individuals | 1,686 | 430 | 1,256 | 819 | 437 |
| Males | 5,948 | — | — | 1,905 | — |
| Females | 3,994 | — | — | 1,626 | — |
| Whites | 7,614 | 2,845 | 4,769 | 2,258 | 2,511 |
| Blacks | 2,185 | 675 | 1,510 | 1,201 | 309 |
| | | | *(percent)* | | |
| EEI index | 11.5% | 13.7% | 10.6% | 13.1% | 8.5% |
| Family heads | 13.7 | 17.8 | 11.9 | 15.1 | 9.6 |
| Wives | 6.3 | 6.7 | 6.1 | 7.0 | 5.4 |
| Other relatives | 7.8 | 8.2 | 7.6 | 9.4 | 6.2 |
| Unrelated individuals | 19.0 | 23.1 | 17.9 | 19.0 | 16.1 |
| Males | 11.3 | — | — | 12.0 | — |
| Females | 11.9 | — | — | 14.6 | — |
| Whites | 10.0 | 12.0 | 9.0 | 10.5 | 8.0 |
| Blacks | 25.2 | 32.4 | 22.9 | 23.8 | 20.1 |
| Male    whites | 9.9 | — | — | 10.0 | — |
|       blacks | 24.7 | — | — | 21.8 | — |
| Female    whites | 10.0 | — | — | 11.2 | — |
|       blacks | 25.8 | — | — | 26.0 | — |

In terms of achieving adequate employment and earnings or of approaching greater equality with whites, blacks are relatively better off in the central city than in nonmetropolitan areas. Among blacks outside SMSAs, the EEI index was 32 percent; in the central city it was 24 percent and in the suburbs, 20 percent.

Another important difference is the high incidence of female-headed families in the central city. While central cities contained

**Table 9. Distribution of Inadequate Employment and Earnings by Area of Residence, March 1972**

| | U.S. Total | Outside SMSA | SMSA | Central City | Suburban Ring |
|---|---|---|---|---|---|
| Family heads | 58.7% | 65.3% | 55.1% | 53.4% | 57.1% |
| White females | (9.0) | — | — | (8.6) | — |
| Black females | (4.5) | — | — | (7.9) | — |
| Wives | 12.2 | 11.9 | 12.4 | 10.9 | 14.3 |
| Other relatives | 12.1 | 10.7 | 12.8 | 12.5 | 13.2 |
| Unrelated individuals | 17.0 | 12.1 | 19.7 | 23.2 | 15.4 |
| Males | 59.8 | — | — | 54.0 | — |
| Females | 40.2 | — | — | 46.0 | — |
| Whites | 76.6 | 79.8 | 74.8 | 63.9 | 88.3 |
| Blacks | 22.0 | 18.9 | 23.7 | 34.0 | 10.9 |
| Unemployed | 27.5 | 20.0 | 31.6 | 32.0 | 31.2 |
| Discouraged | 5.5 | 6.0 | 5.1 | 5.2 | 5.1 |
| Low-paid fully-employed heads | 20.9 | 29.7 | 16.0 | 15.8 | 16.2 |
| Other low-earning heads | 35.0 | 33.9 | 35.6 | 36.1 | 35.0 |
| Employed part-time involuntarily | 11.2 | 10.4 | 11.6 | 10.9 | 12.6 |

only three-tenths of all family heads, they accounted for 45 percent of all female family heads who, in turn, accounted for 16.5 percent of persons with inadequate employment and earnings in central cities (compared with 11.8 percent elsewhere). Women made up 54.2 percent of the central city population, compared with 52.5 percent elsewhere. Since the labor force participation rate of central city females was higher—45.6 percent compared with 43.4 percent in other areas—women accounted for 41.3 percent of the labor forces in the central city, but 37.8 percent of those in the non-central city areas.

A final difference is the concentration of unrelated individuals in the central cities. With 32 percent of the adult population, central cities contained 46 percent of all unrelated individuals. The inadequacy rate was slightly higher in the central city than in the suburbs, but lower than outside the SMSAs. Overall, unrelated individuals in the central city accounted for 49 percent of all unrelated individuals with inadequate employment and earnings.

None of these patterns should be surprising to students of urban problems. Nevertheless, these facts bear repetition because of their significance in the analysis of ghetto subemployment. There are consistent patterns of variation, with low earnings among family heads the major problem in nonmetropolitan areas, and the difficulties of female family heads and unrelated individuals becoming more predominant in the central cities. Urban poverty areas have a still greater concentration of unrelated individuals, females, and blacks. Ghetto problems are part of a spectrum, differing in type and intensity from those of other areas. However, those in the ghettoes account for only a minority of all persons with inadequate employment and earnings.

## The Important Findings

The data for March 1972 suggest that the proposed EEI is a reasonable measure of employment and earnings difficulties. Groups with the most questionable needs were excluded, and the application of the upper income limit was effective in weeding out others who may have had employment difficulties, but not acute income problems. The low average household income of the individuals counted in the EEI and the high proportion of these who were classified as poor are proof that the most disadvantaged were counted. It might, in fact, be argued that the restrictive definitions underestimated the extent of employment and earnings inadequacy. At any rate, the data demonstrate the usefulness of the index and yield a number of significant insights.

1. Inadequate employment and earnings are pervasive, with one in nine actual or would-be labor force participants throughout the nation the victims of one or more of the labor market problems measured by the EEI. These problems vary in type and intensity from area to area and from group to group, but no segment of the population is exempt.

2. Based on their household income in the previous year, many unemployed hardly could be considered needy. Because the Current Population Survey unemployment rate does not count many who experience labor market problems but includes some relatively affluent with temporary problems, it leaves much to be desired as a barometer of need.

3. Low earnings is a more widespread problem than unemployment, discouragement, and involuntary part-time work. Even "full" employment is no guarantee of an adequate income. And as the large number of intermittently working poor suggests, many persons not counted as unemployed, discouraged, or working part-time involuntarily during any survey week face compound problems of low and frequently interrupted earnings.

4. Racial inadequacy differentials are very significant. A fourth of black labor force participants and would-be workers—and half of black family heads in nonmetropolitan areas—had inadequate employment and earnings. To make matters worse, the mean income was lower and the incidence of poverty higher for the blacks than for the whites in the EEI.

5. In light of its application to March 1972 data, several revisions in the definition of the EEI index might be considered.

   a. The involuntary part-time category might be excluded from the needs measure since those in this group had a relatively high average income and low incidence of poverty, while those having the most severe problems were included in the "other low-earning heads" category.

b. All persons—not just family heads—working full-time, full-year at a poverty level wage might be included in the EEI as long as the family upper income limits are applied.

c. The upper and lower income bounds could be refined. The poverty thresholds for nonmetropolitan areas may not realistically reflect cost-of-living differences relative to metropolitan areas. For the upper bound, it might be more desirable to use median rather than mean incomes, or to use a derived standard-of-living measure based on consumer needs. Still other alternatives are possible and would determine the inclusiveness of the measure.

Yet, as it stands, the EEI index is a comprehensive and realistic measure. Reasonable adjustments in definition are not likely to alter significantly the findings for March 1972. And whatever changes are made, an index of this type will be extremely helpful in interpreting employment and earnings conditions and their relation to labor force problems.

# 4

## Changes in the Index, 1968–1972

The EEI can also serve as a cyclical and secular measure of worker welfare. Current Population Survey data permit the calculation of the EEI index back to March 1968. While the five observations for the years 1968 through 1972 are hardly adequate for conclusive time series analysis, the period is an especially instructive one. The secular rise in the number of females in the labor force continued, as did the decline in male participation rates. These four years also witnessed a near doubling of welfare rolls, providing more income alternatives to work. Baffling to analysts, as well as to policymakers and the victims themselves, was the imperviousness of certain structural problems to tight labor markets and the unpredictable relationship which arose between unemployment and inflation. Perhaps most significant, however, was the dramatic cyclical change. In 1968 and 1969, the average rate of unemployment fell to its lowest monthly level (3.3 percent) since the Korean War. With the recession beginning at the end of 1969, the rate of unemployment rose to an average of 4.9 percent in 1970 and 5.9 percent in 1971, recovering sluggishly in 1972 to 5.6 percent. In 1968, there was an average of 2.8 million unemployed but this figure rose to 5.0 million in 1971. Going from a peak to a trough, the 1968 and 1972 data provide the opportunity to observe patterns of change in the EEI over the business cycle.

## The Difficulties of Interpretation

With only five observations, it is an impossible task to distinguish among random fluctuations, cyclical changes, and longer-run trends. The level and composition of the EEI index for any year may be significantly affected by erratic events and sampling errors. The employment status data of the March Current Population Survey are only a snapshot of conditions prevailing in a single week. The standard error for the unemployment rate is about 90,000, and the magnitude of the standard errors for the other components of the EEI index have not been verified, but may be considerable. In addition to sampling variability, random events may have significant impacts. Seasonal factors may have an abnormal impact, or a number of servicemen may be released into the civilian labor force, raising unemployment rates and changing other totals. Because the EEI is a composite index, combining five conceptually distinct labor market pathologies and measures, these random and sampling errors are difficult to disentangle and are undoubtedly large. A number of other technical matters must be considered before year-to-year changes are assessed.

1. The upper and lower income bounds increase over time, but at different rates. The minimum adequacy standards in the EEI—the annual poverty thresholds—are estimates of the income needed to provide a minimum diet and other essentials. As prices rise, these thresholds are raised to meet rising costs of living. No adjustments were made, however, in poverty thresholds in light of changing societal standards. On the other hand, the upper bounds used in the EEI to screen out members of households with more than "adequate" income are *relative* rather than *absolute* standards—the mean incomes for families or unrelated individuals in metropolitan or nonmetropolitan areas. To illustrate this difference, the poverty threshold for a nonfarm family of four rose by 21 percent between 1968 and 1972, while the mean income of families in metropolitan areas rose 32 percent.

There is no reason why the upper and lower adequacy standards have to both be either absolute or relative, although such symmetry would probably simplify interpretation. Since the EEI approach is not symmetrical, it is important to test the longer-term impact of the definitions adopted for the survey. A separate tabulation was prepared for March 1972, using upper adequacy bounds which were calculated by adjusting 1967 mean income levels for the 21 percent cost-of-living increase reflected in the rising poverty thresholds. The resulting lower thresholds screened out more individuals and reduced by 4 percent the number of persons counted as having inadequate employment and earnings. A difference of this magnitude over the course of four years may not be considered significant, but it would cumulate over a longer period. It would appear desirable, therefore, to develop an absolute upper standard or a relative lower standard to improve the value of the EEI index as a tool for measuring longer-run change.

2. In order to focus on persons with greatest need, the EEI index excludes students and the elderly and does not count wives and other relatives among those in the low earnings categories. As a result, changes in the composition of the labor force have an impact on the EEI. Between March 1968 and 1972, wives and other relatives increased from 38.8 to 40.3 percent of the labor force, as the percentage of family heads fell from 51.9 to 49.3. Since secondary participants have much lower EEI indices, their increasing proportion in the labor force reduced the anticipated number with inadequate employment and earnings by 4 percent over the four-year period. (The use of an absolute rather than relative upper income bound would have had approximately the same effect, but in the opposite direction. If compensatory adjustments were made, they would cancel each other, and changes in the EEI index between 1968 and 1972 would remain roughly the same as those tabulated.)

3. Metropolitan and nonmetropolitan areas were redefined after the 1970 Census, increasing the number of SMSAs; these new definitions were used in the March 1972 CPS. The nonmetropolitan share of the EEI total labor force remained unchanged at 34.2 percent between 1968 and 1971, but the fewer redefined nonmetropolitan areas in the March 1972 CPS accounted for only 30.1 percent of the labor force. Analysis of EEI changes inside and outside SMSAs must therefore be limited to the 1968 to 1971 period or, in the future, to the years beginning in 1972.

4. There are some conceptual problems in interpreting business cycle changes. The EEI's employment-related components—unemployment, discouragement, and involuntary part-time employment—are based on the current status in the survey week. The earnings-related components are based on income over the preceding 12 months, assuming that the working poor in the previous year have a high probability of remaining poor. Labor market changes are picked up immediately in the employment-related segments, but the earnings impacts lag, as they affect annual averages more gradually. Since there are twice as many low earners as unemployed in the EEI, the inadequacy index will be less responsive to cyclical changes than the unemployment rate.

Rising unemployment increases this component, but it would also tend to reduce, with some lag, the number of persons employed full-time, full-year at poverty-level wages. The number of "other low-earning household heads" would be influenced by conflicting forces. On the one hand, this category would expand in periods of high unemployment because more people would experience intermittent idleness and therefore lower annual earnings. On the other hand, more from this group would be currently unemployed and picked up in this category.

There are other factors that tend to increase the cyclical sensitivity of the EEI. Employed wives and other relatives with low earnings are excluded from the EEI measure even if their income is vital to the family. But if they lose their jobs or are put on part-time schedules because of slack demand, then they are counted.

The analysis of year-to-year changes in the EEI is thus a complex process. There is no way to estimate the extent that random events or standard errors have affected the totals and especially disaggregated components. The only recourse is to determine whether the data make sense and move in consistent and expected patterns. If the data withstand such scrutiny, then an assessment of cyclical changes and indications of longer run developments may be in order, although the conclusions must be considered tentative.

## Consistency and Predictability

Changes in the EEI and its components between 1968 and 1972 were reasonable and consistent with expectations. As a result of the recession, the number of persons with inadequate employment and earnings increased by almost two million (table 10). Reacting to fluctuations within this period, the EEI declined between 1968 and 1969 as aggregate unemployment fell, rose between 1969 and 1971, and declined slightly between 1971 and 1972. However, the oscillations were much less pronounced than in unemployment. The Current Population Survey unemployment rate fell by 8 percent between March 1968 and March 1969 while the EEI index declined by 6 percent; unemployment rose 37 percent between March 1970 and March 1971 and the EEI went up by 16 percent (table 11).

While EEI unemployment fluctuated significantly, the number of low-paid, fully-employed heads varied inversely as low wage workers lost or gained stable jobs (chart 1). In March 1969, when the unemployed in the EEI accounted for 2.0 percent of the adjusted labor force, fully-employed low-earners represented 3.2 percent. By March 1971, the EEI unemployed had risen to 3.3 percent while the fully-employed component had declined to 2.4 percent. The "other low-paid heads" category varied directly with unemployment, but with a one-year lag.

Given these cyclical relationships, it would be expected that over the entire period of rising unemployment, the low-paid, fully-employed category would decline while the other low earning category would increase. This occurred, with the former falling

**Table 10. Inadequate Employment and Earnings, 1968–1972**

|  | 1968 | 1969 | 1970 | 1971 | 1972 |
|---|---|---|---|---|---|
|  | *(in thousands)* | | | | |
| Adjusted labor force | 77,941 | 79,466 | 82,151 | 83,324 | 86,122 |
| Total with inadequate | | | | | |
|   employment and earnings | 8,099 | 7,752 | 8,184 | 9,647 | 9,942 |
|     Unemployed | 1,589 | 1,427 | 1,835 | 2,763 | 2,731 |
|     Discouraged | 383 | 136 | 357 | 484 | 542 |
|     Low-paid fully | | | | | |
|       employed heads | 2,536 | 2,521 | 2,179 | 2,035 | 2,078 |
|     Other low-paid heads | 2,660 | 2,792 | 2,823 | 3,136 | 3,478 |
|     Employed part-time | | | | | |
|       involuntarily | 932 | 876 | 990 | 1,229 | 1,113 |
| EEI index | 10.4% | 9.8% | 10.0% | 11.6% | 11.5% |

**Table 11. Changes in Unemployment and EEI Rates, 1968–1972**

| | Level | | | | | Change | | | |
|---|---|---|---|---|---|---|---|---|---|
| | 1968 | 1969 | 1970 | 1971 | 1972 | 1968–69 | 1969–70 | 1970–71 | 1971–72 |
| CPS unemployment rate | 3.8% | 3.5% | 4.6% | 6.3% | 6.1% | -8% | 31% | 37% | -3% |
| Unemployment component of subemployed as percent of adjusted labor force | 3.1 | 2.7 | 3.7 | 5.1 | 4.9 | -10 | 35 | 38 | -4 |
| Unemployment component of EEI as percent of adjusted labor force | 2.0 | 1.8 | 2.2 | 3.3 | 3.2 | -11 | 24 | 48 | -4 |
| EEI index | 10.4 | 9.8 | 10.0 | 11.6 | 11.5 | -6 | 2 | 16 | -1 |

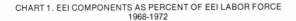

CHART 1. EEI COMPONENTS AS PERCENT OF EEI LABOR FORCE
1968-1972

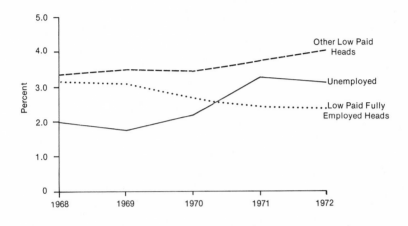

from 31 to 21 percent of the total, and the latter rising from 33 to 35 percent (chart 2).

The same general patterns of change prevailed for most family, sex, race, and area of residence groups (chart 3). Among family heads, for instance, the inadequacy rate declined in 1969, rose modestly in 1970, significantly in 1971, and then remained relatively stable in 1972. In both 1968 and 1972, one of every ten family heads in the labor force was in the low earnings group; the rise in the EEI index for family heads from 12.4 to 13.7 percent between the two years resulted entirely from increasing joblessness. During the 1968–1972 period, inadequacy increased more among females than males because a larger percentage were in the employment-related categories, which are more subject to cyclical fluctuations. Inadequacy also rose much more in metropolitan than in nonmetropolitan areas.

The only exception to the above EEI pattern was unrelated individuals. Their EEI index declined from 18.4 percent in 1968 to 17.0 percent in 1970, largely due to a marked decline in the fully-employed, low-earners category. There is no way to know whether

73

CHART 2.  DISTRIBUTION OF EEI
1968-1972

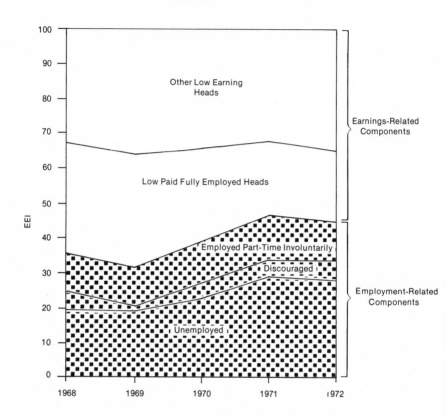

this was an aberration in the estimates or a real phenomenon which could be explained by other factors. The fluctuations of the other EEI components were, however, consistent with expected patterns of change.

### Need and the Level of Unemployment

Given a basic understanding of the factors affecting cyclical and longer run changes in the EEI and of the problems involved in interpretation, the index may be used for a number of purposes. One is to determine the impact of the business cycle upon needs.

Comparison of the EEIs for different groups in March 1971 and March 1969—the high and low unemployment points in the EEI series—reveals that inadequacy did not increase as rapidly as unemployment. While the number of unemployed (not including students 16 to 21 years of age and persons 65 and over) increased 95 percent in the period between the two years, the number counted as having inadequate employment and earnings rose by a fourth (table 12). Rising unemployment meant more discouraged, part-time, and intermittently employed workers with low earnings, but these increases were offset somewhat by the decline in the number of fully-employed household heads and by the fact that many among the added persons with employment problems were members of households with above average incomes in the previous year. The estimated mean household income of the additional unemployed was $10,000, so that many were screened out in deriving the EEI. The number of unemployed excluded by the upper income bound in 1971 amounted to 1.5 million, double the number two years earlier.

Females, whites, metropolitan residents, and wives and other relatives bore a disproportionate burden of the EEI increase between 1969 and 1971 because persons added to the EEI in the slack labor market were drawn from the more "advantaged" segments of the labor force. White wives and other relatives accounted for a fifth of the EEI, but they constituted 45 percent of the total rise between the subsequent two years. Inadequacy among black male family heads actually declined, and female family heads represented the same proportion of the EEI in both 1969 and 1971.

Among all groups, the recession added many to the EEI who had higher incomes than those who were included during a tight labor market period. The mean income of family heads included in the EEI between 1969 and 1971 was $7,900, or 72 percent above the average for the family heads included in 1969. The additional unrelated individuals had an estimated average income of $3,300, or nearly two and a half times the mean for that EEI group two years earlier. In 1969, 49 percent of those with inadequate employment were poor, compared with 41 percent of those counted in the 1971 EEI.

75

CHART 3. DISTRIBUTION OF EEI

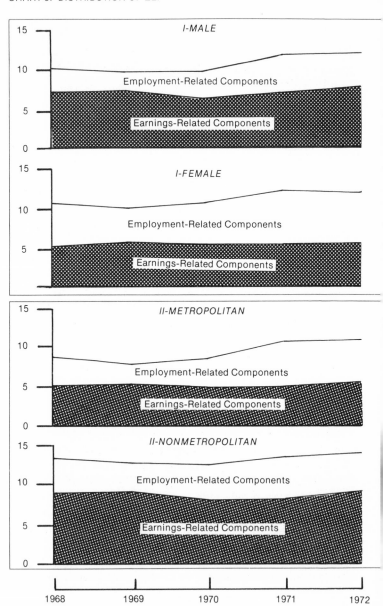

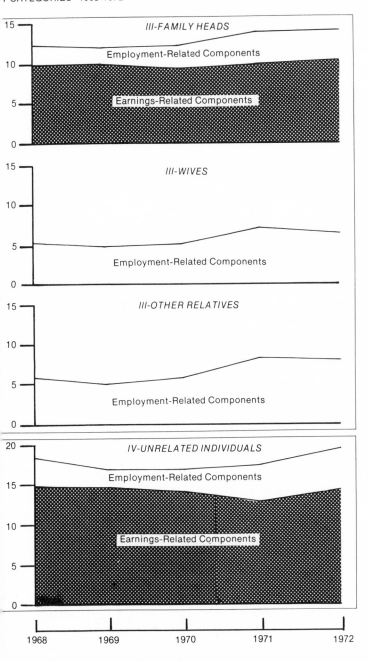

III-FAMILY HEADS

Employment-Related Components

Earnings-Related Components

III-WIVES

Employment-Related Components

III-OTHER RELATIVES

Employment-Related Components

IV-UNRELATED INDIVIDUALS

Employment-Related Components

Earnings-Related Components

1968    1969    1970    1971    1972

Table 12. Comparative Distribution of Unemployment* and Inadequacy, 1969 and 1971

| | % of 1969 EEI | % of 1971 EEI | % of Increment in EEI 1969–1971 | % of 1969 Unemployed | % of 1971 Unemployed | % of Increment for Unemployed 1969–1971 |
|---|---|---|---|---|---|---|
| Male | 61.0 | 59.3 | 52.1 | 50.3 | 57.3 | 64.7 |
| Female | 39.0 | 40.7 | 47.9 | 49.7 | 42.7 | 35.3 |
| White | 74.1 | 77.0 | 88.9 | 79.5 | 83.0 | 86.7 |
| Black | 24.5 | 21.7 | 10.5 | 19.7 | 15.7 | 11.5 |
| Metropolitan | 55.0 | 60.4 | 82.8 | 61.7 | 65.6 | 69.7 |
| Nonmetropolitan | 45.0 | 39.6 | 17.2 | 38.3 | 34.4 | 30.3 |
| Family heads | 64.1 | 59.1 | 39.0 | 32.5 | 35.6 | 39.0 |
| Wives | 10.6 | 13.6 | 25.9 | 28.5 | 24.2 | 19.7 |
| Other relatives | 8.5 | 12.3 | 27.7 | 31.4 | 29.3 | 27.0 |
| Unrelated individuals | 16.8 | 15.0 | 7.4 | 7.6 | 10.9 | 14.4 |
| White males | 46.9 | 47.1 | 47.8 | 41.3 | 48.5 | 56.1 |
| Family heads | 39.3 | 36.6 | 25.6 | 23.6 | 27.0 | 30.6 |
| Other relatives | 3.3 | 5.6 | 15.0 | 14.6 | 16.0 | 17.1 |
| Unrelated individuals | 4.3 | 4.9 | 7.1 | 3.0 | 5.6 | 8.4 |
| White females | 27.3 | 30.0 | 41.2 | 38.2 | 34.5 | 30.6 |
| Family heads | 8.8 | 9.1 | 10.3 | 3.3 | 3.3 | 3.2 |
| Wives | 8.3 | 11.1 | 22.6 | 23.9 | 20.9 | 17.7 |
| Other relatives | 1.9 | 3.0 | 7.2 | 8.3 | 7.2 | 6.1 |
| Unrelated individuals | 8.3 | 6.9 | 1.1 | 2.8 | 2.2 | 2.6 |

| | | | | | |
|---|---|---|---|---|---|
| Black males | 13.1 | 11.5 | 4.0 | 8.0 | 8.1 | 7.5 |
| Family heads | 9.8 | 7.7 | -0.7 | 3.7 | 3.2 | 2.6 |
| Other relatives | 1.8 | 2.2 | 3.9 | 4.0 | 3.6 | 3.2 |
| Unrelated individuals | 1.6 | 1.6 | 1.5 | 1.0 | 1.3 | 1.7 |
| Black females | 11.4 | 10.3 | 5.8 | 11.1 | 7.6 | 4.0 |
| Family heads | 5.4 | 5.0 | 3.6 | 1.7 | 1.7 | 1.7 |
| Wives | 2.2 | 2.3 | 2.5 | 4.4 | 3.0 | 1.7 |
| Other relatives | 1.5 | 1.5 | 1.5 | 4.2 | 2.3 | 0.3 |
| Unrelated individuals | 2.3 | 1.4 | -1.8 | 0.8 | 0.6 | 0.3 |
| SMSA whites | 39.5 | 46.0 | 72.3 | 47.0 | 52.7 | 58.8 |
| Family heads | 23.5 | 24.9 | 30.7 | 14.8 | 18.9 | 23.3 |
| Wives | 4.4 | 7.0 | 17.6 | 13.9 | 12.8 | 11.6 |
| Other relatives | 3.1 | 5.2 | 14.0 | 14.2 | 14.0 | 13.8 |
| Unrelated individuals | 8.6 | 8.8 | 10.0 | 4.1 | 7.0 | 10.1 |
| SMSA blacks | 14.6 | 13.7 | 9.8 | 14.3 | 12.0 | 9.7 |
| Family heads | 8.9 | 7.7 | 3.1 | 4.0 | 3.9 | 3.8 |
| Wives | 1.5 | 1.5 | 1.4 | 3.7 | 2.5 | 1.1 |
| Other relatives | 1.7 | 2.4 | 5.1 | 5.1 | 4.2 | 3.3 |
| Unrelated individuals | 2.5 | 2.1 | 0.2 | 1.5 | 1.5 | 1.5 |
| Non-SMSA whites | 34.6 | 31.1 | 16.6 | 32.5 | 30.3 | 28.0 |
| Family heads | 24.5 | 20.8 | 5.3 | 12.1 | 11.4 | 10.6 |
| Wives | 3.9 | 4.1 | 5.0 | 10.0 | 8.1 | 6.1 |
| Other relatives | 2.2 | 3.3 | 8.1 | 8.7 | 9.1 | 9.4 |
| Unrelated individuals | 4.1 | 2.9 | -1.8 | 1.7 | 1.8 | 1.9 |
| Non-SMSA blacks | 9.9 | 8.1 | 0.7 | 5.4 | 3.7 | 1.8 |
| Family heads | 6.3 | 5.0 | -0.2 | 1.4 | 1.0 | 0.6 |
| Wives | 0.7 | 0.8 | 1.1 | 0.6 | 0.6 | 0.6 |
| Other relatives | 1.5 | 1.3 | 0.2 | 3.1 | 1.7 | 0.2 |
| Unrelated individuals | 1.3 | 0.9 | -0.6 | 0.3 | 0.4 | 0.5 |

*Excludes 16- to 21-year-olds in school and individuals 65 and over but without upper income screen.

In summary, the EEI fluctuates less than the unemployment rate, reflecting the fact that in a recession, many of those without jobs are secondary workers or persons with adequate past or supplementary income. The EEI does rise in a slack labor market, but those who are added are usually better off than those who previously had inadequate employment and earnings and whose position undoubtedly grows worse.

## Black/White Differentials

While it is impossible to separate longer trends from cyclical fluctuations with only five observations, the data suggest that there may have been both absolute and relative declines in inadequacy among blacks. In March 1968, the black EEI was 27.2 percent; by March 1972, it had fallen to 25.2 percent (table 13). Over the same period, the index for whites rose from 8.4 percent to 10.0 percent, so that the ratio of black to white EEI declined from 3.2 to 2.5.

These apparent gains were realized despite the fact that the nonwhite Current Population Survey unemployment rate rose by two-thirds, from 6.1 to 10.4 percent between March 1968 and March 1972, while the nonwhite/white unemployment ratio also rose slightly from 1.8 to 1.9. One reason why the EEI results were more favorable to blacks was that the adjusted unemployment rate used in calculating subemployment and inadequacy excluded students 16 to 21 years of age and older persons. This adjusted rate increased more for whites than for blacks between March 1968 and 1972. The CPS-measured changes reflected increasing black teenage employment problems, but the EEI gives these less weight.

The declining percentage of black males in the low earnings categories was the major factor contributing to the dropping of their EEI rates. Where 19.4 percent of black male labor force participants in March 1968 earned less than poverty wages in the previous year, 14.5 percent had this problem in March 1972. The incidence of low earnings increased for white males over the same period. The improvement was less for black females, but for both

**Table 13. Black and White EEI, 1968–1972**

|  | 1968 | 1969 | 1970 | 1971 | 1972 |
|---|---|---|---|---|---|
| *EEI Index* | | | | | |
| Blacks | 27.2 | 23.9 | 23.7 | 25.2 | 25.2 |
|     Males | 26.7 | 22.9 | 22.8 | 24.0 | 24.7 |
|     Females | 27.7 | 25.1 | 24.9 | 26.7 | 25.8 |
| Whites | 8.4 | 8.1 | 8.3 | 10.0 | 10.0 |
|     Males | 8.4 | 8.2 | 8.1 | 9.9 | 9.9 |
|     Females | 8.6 | 8.1 | 8.7 | 10.3 | 10.0 |
| Metropolitan | | | | | |
|     Blacks | 22.7 | 19.2 | 19.4 | 21.5 | 22.9 |
|     Whites | 7.0 | 6.7 | 7.1 | 9.2 | 9.0 |
| Nonmetropolitan | | | | | |
|     Blacks | 38.4 | 37.2 | 36.4 | 35.4 | 32.4 |
|     Whites | 11.1 | 10.8 | 10.6 | 11.5 | 12.0 |
| *Employment components* (unemployment, discouragement, part-time employment rates) | | | | | |
| Blacks | 9.8 | 7.4 | 9.6 | 11.1 | 11.8 |
|     Males | 7.3 | 5.4 | 7.6 | 9.1 | 10.3 |
|     Females | 13.1 | 10.0 | 12.0 | 13.7 | 13.7 |
| Whites | 3.0 | 2.6 | 3.2 | 4.7 | 4.3 |
|     Males | 2.3 | 1.9 | 2.6 | 3.9 | 3.6 |
|     Females | 4.2 | 3.7 | 4.2 | 6.0 | 5.5 |
| Metropolitan | | | | | |
|     Blacks | 8.7 | 6.4 | 8.2 | 10.4 | 11.6 |
|     Whites | 2.8 | 2.3 | 3.0 | 4.8 | 4.3 |
| Nonmetropolitan | | | | | |
|     Blacks | 12.7 | 10.3 | 13.6 | 13.2 | 12.1 |
|     Whites | 3.5 | 3.1 | 3.7 | 4.5 | 4.4 |
| *Low earnings components* | | | | | |
| Blacks | 17.3 | 16.4 | 14.2 | 14.1 | 13.4 |
|     Males | 19.4 | 17.5 | 15.2 | 14.9 | 14.5 |
|     Females | 14.6 | 15.1 | 12.9 | 13.1 | 12.1 |
| Whites | 5.4 | 5.5 | 5.1 | 5.3 | 5.7 |
|     Males | 6.0 | 6.2 | 5.5 | 5.9 | 6.4 |
|     Females | 4.4 | 4.4 | 4.4 | 4.3 | 4.4 |
| Metropolitan | | | | | |
|     Blacks | 14.0 | 12.8 | 11.2 | 11.2 | 11.2 |
|     Whites | 4.3 | 4.4 | 4.2 | 4.4 | 4.7 |
| Nonmetropolitan | | | | | |
|     Blacks | 25.6 | 26.8 | 22.8 | 22.2 | 20.3 |
|     Whites | 7.6 | 7.6 | 6.9 | 7.0 | 7.6 |

sexes there was a decline in low earners from 17.4 to 13.4 percent of the labor force, compared with an increase from 5.4 to 5.7 percent for whites (chart 4).

Several factors other than actual improvements in the employment and earnings status of blacks may have contributed to their declining EEI. For one thing, the proportion of black labor force participants residing in nonmetropolitan areas declined from 28.4 percent in 1968 to 26.5 percent in 1971, while the percentage for whites actually increased slightly. If the nonmetropolitan black labor force had grown at the same rate as the total black labor force, there would have been 95,000 more black workers outside the SMSAs in 1971. The migrants may be no better off in real terms, even though their earnings raised them above the urban poverty thresholds; they therefore were not counted in the EEI. Some migrants may also either "disappear" into street life or leave the labor force for welfare or illicit activities. Yet, even the most extreme assumptions do not explain the overall fall in inadequate employment and earnings among blacks. If all of the 95,000 black labor force participants who shifted area of residence had previously been in the EEI, and if all of them either got jobs which left them no better off in real terms, or if they became "invisible," the index would have been understated in 1971 by only a percentage point, leaving another percentage point decline in black EEI due to real and not "statistical" improvements.

A more important factor was the declining labor force participation rate of blacks. As defined in the EEI index, the black male participation rate fell from 77.3 percent in 1968 to 73.0 percent in 1972, while the white male rate fell 0.4 percentage points to 78.9 percent. Among black women, the rate declined from 49.7 to 49.3 percent while it rose among white women from 40.6 to 43.3. If black participation had changed by the same amount as for whites, there would have been roughly half a million more black labor force participants in 1972. If it is assumed that a large percentage of the "dropouts" would have joined the 2.2 million blacks with inadequate employment and earnings in that year, the impact would have been significant. Still, it appears that the chances of black labor force participants being included in the EEI has declined during the four-year period.

CHART 4. TRENDS OF CHANGE IN BLACK AND WHITE EEI
1968-1972

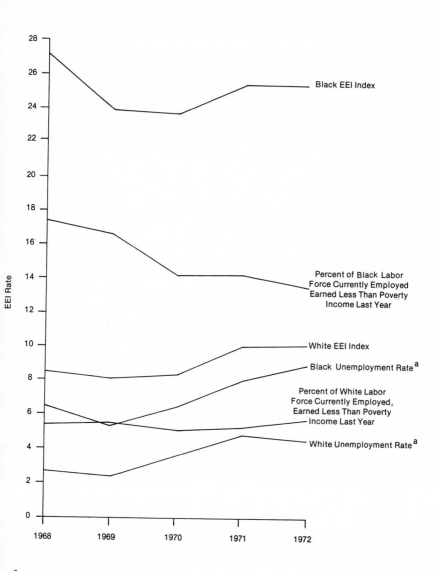

$^a$Unemployment Rate Excludes 16- to 21-year-old Students and
Persons 65 and Over.

## The EEI As A Measure of Change

Derivation and analysis of the EEI for March 1968 through 1972 demonstrate its potential as well as limitations as a social indicator. Changes from year to year are consistent with expectations, and predictable patterns seem to emerge. Inadequacy is related to conventional unemployment rates, but the fluctuations are much less dramatic because a larger proportion of the unemployed are screened out as the rate rises and because some of the unemployed are drawn from the ranks of the otherwise inadequately employed. When the data are analyzed for different groups, the same patterns emerge, suggesting that erratic or exogenous factors are not distorting the totals. Further analysis is needed to determine standard errors and other factors which may have an influence on EEI levels, but the regularity of the changes between 1968 and 1972 should bolster confidence in the measure and help put the 1972 data in perspective.

Clearly, however, the EEI must be used carefully in assessing changes over time. It is a complex index, mixing time frames and encompassing a number of different problems which are measured in different ways. The definition is asymmetric with respect to certain groups such as wives and other relatives, so that longer run changes in participation patterns alter the index. The upper and lower standards of adequacy vary at different rates, making it difficult to separate absolute and relative gains. However, if used carefully, the EEI can provide new perspectives on some important developments over time. For instance, analysis of EEI changes between 1969 and 1971 demonstrated that many of the recession's victims were secondary workers and persons from households with more than adequate incomes in the previous year. Likewise, analysis of the data for 1968 through 1972 suggested that the relative and absolute status of blacks in the labor force improved. Disturbingly high racial differentials persisted, but the percentage of blacks in low-paying or intermittent jobs steadily declined over the four-year period, while inadequacy among whites increased.

The EEI concept is a potentially useful tool for assessing labor market changes, although it requires much rigorous technical work. Considering the undoubtedly large standard errors in the interrelated component variables, the data must be handled with extreme care. Precision will remain elusive in considering diverse pathologies and in setting standards of adequacy. The realistic goal is the derivation of a reasonable and general measure which provides new perspective and insights into labor market behavior.

# 5

## Policy Implications

The EEI index provides a needed conceptual link between employment and earnings problems, creating a "needs" measure by screening *out* the unemployed with above average income and by screening *in* the working poor who are heads of families and discouraged workers who are excluded from the Current Population Survey labor force statistics. The index provides some new perspectives on labor market conditions and patterns, exposing hidden problems and providing insights on changes over time. To be effective, however, the EEI index must do more than describe evolving conditions in light of emerging economic concepts; it must also be useful in addressing current policy issues and concerns.

There are dangers, however, in applying the index before it is well tested and verified. One reason for the halting progress in developing a subemployment measure has been the irresistible temptation to draw conclusions on the basis of tentative findings. Hastily prepared estimates released in 1967 were used to justify ghetto development efforts. Critics of these policies attacked and discredited the subemployment concept. Once the ghetto programs had been launched, the impetus for further development of the measure was dissipated.

The primary goal of the present analysis was to design a measure which could be refined and adopted on a sustained basis, not to espouse ad hoc policies or to tie the EEI to predetermined purposes. But the potential policy implications and applications of an inadequacy index are clear. The measure cuts through a thicket of related issues, and although the rigor with which it is applied leaves much to be desired, it helps to identify, organize, and interpret a variety of factors which might otherwise be ignored and misunderstood. The proposed measure provides perspectives on a number of basic social problems, as the following examples suggest.

## Continuing Structural Problems

Public concern with the state of the labor market tends to fluctuate with the rate of unemployment. When joblessness increases, pressures mount for measures to support the unemployed and to stimulate employment growth. When the labor market is tight, the cries for action decrease. Consensus on long range efforts to help those who have problems even in a healthy economy is hard to obtain, partially because of the belief that when the unemployment rate declines to a "reasonable" level, all is well.

The EEI index tells a different story; the number of persons with severe needs does not fluctuate widely over the business cycle, and inadequate employment and earnings remain a continuing problem for millions even when there is "full employment." When the CPS unemployment rate had declined to 3.5 percent in March 1969, nearly one in every ten persons in the adjusted labor force had inadequate employment and earnings. The rise in unemployment between 1969 and 1971 certainly intensified conditions for those at the end of the labor queue, and added to the EEI total. While the unemployment rate rose by four-fifths, the EEI rose only a fourth as much.

Employment and earnings inadequacy is a continuing structural problem, and its alleviation requires a long-run commitment to eliminate inequities in the wage structure and in employment practices. The message for policymakers is that inadequacy does not disappear when unemployment declines, and neither should public efforts to combat labor market problems.

87

On the other hand, some may argue from the same evidence that because the EEI index does not increase much when joblessness rises, a higher unemployment rate does not imply greater needs and is therefore tolerable. Such an argument is shortsighted. The increase in the EEI index from 1969 to 1971 may not have been large in percentage terms, but the number of individuals added to the inadequacy total was two-thirds as great as the increase in the number of unemployed. Second, the EEI index was designed to measure more severe problems which tend to fluctuate less than current unemployment measurements. Third, the severity of needs among those with inadequate employment and earnings is intensified by rising unemployment as low-paid, fully-employed workers become low-paid, intermittent workers with reduced earnings. Whether or not inadequacy rises as much as unemployment, millions of people are affected already, and severe problems grow worse. To say that continuing measures are required does not negate the need for and desirability of efforts to combat recessions or to maintain a low equilibrium level of unemployment.

## Unemployment and Inadequacy

Since the Great Depression, labor market measures have focused attention on the availability of work. The implicit assumption has been that almost any job is better than none, and that employment has a higher priority than earnings. Minimum wage legislation has raised the earnings of millions, but increases in the floor and extensions in minimum wage coverage have been modest because of the concern that such a move would also eliminate jobs. Manpower programs for the most part have concentrated on opening jobs for the disadvantaged, even though in many cases wages from these jobs still left the participants below poverty levels.

The validity of these public policy tenets was brought under scrutiny as a result of developments in the 1960s. In the tight labor markets, extensive unemployment continued despite the existence of unfilled jobs requiring few skills. The explanation offered by the dual labor market theory was that bad jobs were linked with unemployment because workers at the end of the labor queue lacked commitment to their low-paying positions, quit frequently, and often turned to alternative sources of income, since low-wage employers failed to exert serious efforts to make their jobs more attractive.

The EEI index which addresses both the earnings and employment dimensions suggests that there is an interrelationship, with earnings problems at least as important as unemployment. In March 1972, there were 2.3 million household heads who had worked full-time, full-year in the previous 12 months but had not earned enough to raise their families out of poverty. Another 3.7 million had worked less than full-time in the previous year and had earned less than a poverty-level income for their households. Only 28 percent of the EEI total were unemployed, with half of these being secondary family earners.

The fully-employed poor have very critical and persistent problems. They are committed workers—almost four-fifths are family heads—and their low earnings have serious consequences for dependents. The chances are minimal for an improvement in jobs and earnings which will substantially better their status; on the contrary, they are haunted by the possibility that unemployment will reduce their already meager earnings. Between March 1969 and March 1971, the number of low-paid, fully-employed heads decreased by half a million, representing mostly declining rather than increasing incomes.

Intermittently employed low earners have even more severe needs. While some have low earnings because of recent entrance into the labor force, two-thirds are family heads for whom the combination of unemployment and low wages reduces average income to an extremely low level. The EEI data suggest the existence of a "secondary" labor market which contains millions of persons.

The EEI index is one way of highlighting the fact that low wages are a serious problem deserving more attention. Raising the minimum wage is one possible policy. But this may also increase unemployment, especially among those at the end of the labor queue. There is ample evidence that more people have gained income than lost their jobs as a result of past increases in the minimum, but the inadequacy total falls by only the net of the two. A more direct way to reduce inadequacy and the EEI is to subsidize wages of low-paid, fully-employed family heads. Considering the extent of the inadequate earnings problem this approach should be considered as an additional tool in the arsenal of needed social legislation.

## Crisis Conditions

The EEI documents the fact that for disadvantaged groups in the population the chances of labor market failure are high, making alternative life styles more attractive than working at legitimate but dead-end jobs. In March 1972, more than two-fifths of all female family heads who were labor force participants had inadequate employment and earnings, and over half of them lived in poverty. Black female family heads were even worse off; their EEI index was a staggering 55 percent, and 69 percent lived in poverty. Married life held little promise, since one of every four black males also had inadequate employment and earnings. With such prospects, it is no wonder that women, especially blacks, turn to welfare in order to support their families. The rise in welfare payments has made dependency more secure and in some cases more remunerative for women with children to support.

Despite the severe problems which exist in the central cities, it is not hard to understand why blacks continue to migrate there from nonmetropolitan areas. In 1972, the inadequacy rate for black family heads outside the SMSAs was 49 percent, compared with 29 percent for the same groups in central cities.

Given these conditions, the discouragement counted by the EEI may be only the tip of the iceberg. Many people are outside the labor force, not because they think work is unavailable but because they know the type jobs for which they will be hired.

## The Distribution of Needs

Because public policy has been concerned primarily with unemployment, assistance has tended to be concentrated on groups having the most serious unemployment problems. There is no equity formula which can precisely distribute public funds and efforts, but if low wages were given equal consideration with job availability, several changes in emphasis might be warranted.

The full-time, full-year working household head who does not earn enough to escape poverty is often ignored. In March 1972, family heads made up 59 percent of persons included in the EEI, although they constituted only 34 percent of the unemployed (excluding students 16 to 21 years of age and persons 65 and over). To the extent the index is an adequate measure of relative need, more emphasis should be focused on low-paid breadwinners.

Nonmetropolitan areas may also be shortchanged. For instance, under the Public Employment Program of 1971, governors and local officials were given grants for the hiring of the unemployed or underemployed in the public sector. The two-part allocational formula used was based on the share and intensity of unemployment. The EEI calculations support the complaint of rural areas that unemployment rates disguised much of their need. In March 1972, nonmetropolitan areas contained 36 percent of all persons with inadequate employment and earnings, but 29 percent of the nonstudent, nonelderly unemployed. If the distribution of public employment funds were based on inadequacy of employment and earnings, nonmetropolitan areas would have received at least a fourth more funds.

Recognizing this problem, the allocational formula for the Comprehensive Employment and Training Act of 1973 would divide up funds according to shares of unemployment and low income populations. But with less than half of poor family heads in the labor force in March 1972, poverty is not a good measure of the need for manpower programs, and neither is the number of unemployed. An index such as the EEI might offer a more equitable basis for the determination of manpower revenue shares.

### Equalizing the Burdens

A critical question is whether concentrated governmental efforts can improve the relative status of the disadvantaged. The EEI index suggests that some progress was made over the 1968–1972 period in helping disadvantaged blacks, whose EEI fell in absolute measures and relative to whites. It is unknown how much of this improvement was due to declining labor force participation among blacks and continued migration to metropolitan areas, as opposed to direct governmental efforts. But the EEI at least raises hopes that some progress has been made and can be continued. This is a more optimistic picture than emerges from the analysis of unemployment rates or average incomes. The reason is that the EEI index concentrates on persons at the end of the labor queue, i.e., those who are likely to qualify for manpower programs and whose wages are likely to be affected by minimum wage laws. The gains being made here will have only a slight effect on the mean and median incomes of blacks and will not necessarily offset other factors such as the increasing problems of black teenagers. Because of its selective focus, a needs index like the EEI provides a better assessment than unemployment rates.

While there are some grounds for optimism, however, there is certainly no justification for "benign neglect." If the rate of improvement in the EEI for blacks between 1968 and 1972 continued unabated while the index for whites remained the same, it would take 38 years to reach parity. This extrapolation may be overly sanguine since black progress was also accompanied by declining labor force participation between 1968 and 1972 which, if continued, would leave only half of adult blacks in the labor force in 2010. The EEI thus provides a sign of progress, as well as proof of the substantial distance which remains to be traveled.

### Adopting an Inadequacy Measure

The major conclusion from the preceding discussion is that an inadequacy measure is feasible and potentially useful for policy formulation. To effectively serve this purpose, however, the index or some better measure must be officially tabulated and published so that it will be in the public domain along with other labor market statistics.

The currently published labor force data are useful tools for the analysis of a wide range of economic issues, but they do not provide a straightforward picture of the number of persons who are unable to attain an adequate standard of living through work. Many persons with patterns of intermittent employment and low earnings are not counted as unemployed at a given point in time.

Others are outside the labor force, having given up the search for a job. Many more are employed, but are earning low wages and are unable to escape poverty despite their best efforts. On the other hand, there are many among the unemployed who are not in economic straits, such as wives, sons, and daughters in affluent families, or family heads able to live off past savings and the income of other family members. In these cases, employment problems are not synonymous with income problems.

An aggregate index is required to isolate and link together the various needs groups, and the EEI is a reasonable approach. Before it can be utilized, however, a number of improvements are needed.

1. Just as low income statistics are provided on the basis of both poverty and "near poverty" thresholds, two EEI indices might be calculated using the separate standards as the lower bounds. This would provide a range of need, increasing the analytical value of the measure while quantifying the implications of differing perceptions of minimal adequacy.

2. The upper income bounds used to screen out persons in households with more than adequate income might be changed, using median rather than mean incomes or some absolute standards adjusted annually for the increased cost of living.

3. Persons employed part-time involuntarily for economic reasons (not included in the "other low-earning heads" category) might be excluded, since their mean household income was found to be relatively high and since most were secondary workers.

4. Persons with low earnings because of voluntary entrance or exit from the labor force during the past year might be screened from the "other low-earning heads" category using the work experience data in the March Current Population Survey.

5. Wives and other relatives working full-time, full-year but earning less than a poverty level wage might be counted in this category, using the upper adequacy screen to weed out those who are not in need.

6. A broader definition of discouragement might be used, even though it might be inconsistent with CPS definitions. When suitable jobs become available, persons not counted as discouraged might prefer other activities which keep them out of the labor market.

These and other improvements in the definition of the inadequacy index will still leave many drawbacks to the application of the EEI and will not resolve the remaining troublesome conceptual issues. But implementation of such a measure does not depend on unanimity or perfection. Other measures, such as the unemployment rate, were introduced and refined over time; they became more meaningful only after a body of analysis emerged which interpreted and applied the statistics. Even greater patience and tolerance is required in developing a needs measure, since the issues to which it is addressed are much more complex.

But clearly the time has come to carry on with the developmental work for an employment and earnings inadequacy index. This fact was recognized by Congress in the Comprehensive Employment and Training Act of 1973, which directed the Department of Labor to "develop preliminary data for an annual statistical measure of labor market related economic hardship in the nation" which would include the components of the EEI. In fulfillment of this mandate, a definition should be agreed upon, data analyzed, and as soon as problems can be ironed out, a new measure should be officially adopted.

## The Underlying Assumptions

Implicit in any social indicator is a "world view"—a set of underlying principles or concepts determining which dimensions of reality and interrelationships will be given emphasis. The preceding arguments for the adoption of the employment and earnings inadequacy index have concentrated on technical issues in its definition and application, while these underlying principles have been discussed only indirectly. In considering the adoption and further refinement of an inadequacy measure, it is important to articulate its implicit conceptual and normative judgments.

1. *The adequacy of employment is as important as its availability.* Rising income and the increasing availability of alternative sources for its supplementation have given workers more freedom than in the past to choose the types of work and pay which are acceptable to them, to leave unsatisfactory jobs, and to weather longer periods of job search. Yet, many persons continue to have limited options. They can usually find jobs, but only those which

pay low wages and offer few opportunities for advancement. For them, full-time, full-year employment does not guarantee a minimally adequate standard of living. One of the fundamental principles underlying the inadequacy concept is that many committed workers employed full-time are not in better situations (and probably worse off) than many persons who experience only short periods of unemployment.

2. *Employment and earnings problems are interrelated and compounded for a significant minority of all workers.* Unemployment, discouragement, and involuntary part-time work are concentrated in low-wage industries and among low-paid workers. Many are trapped in a cycle of limited earnings, minimal job commitment, frequent turnover, both voluntary and involuntary discouragement, and withdrawal from the labor force. The pathologies are interrelated and their consequences cumulatively inimical.

3. *The gravity of employment problems is primarily a determinant of their impact on household income.* The major reason for working is to earn a livelihood, and the major criteria for judging success or failure in the labor market must be the level of earnings and income. While unemployment may have insidious psychic effects, and while interrupted earnings can be a cause of distress at any income level if living standards must be cut back, the underlying judgment of the inadequacy approach is that the person with $10,000 annual income is not as seriously affected by a period of unemployment as the individual earning only $3,000. This does not deny societal responsibility to prevent unemployment and to minimize its impact, but it does assert that those who are worse off are those with the least means to weather adversity.

4. *Priority should be given to helping those with the most severe problems.* Implicit in an inadequacy index which singles out those with the greatest needs is the belief that this group should be of prime concern to public policymakers. Decisions made on the basis of unemployment rates do not always focus on this needs group, because among the unemployed there are many who have only the slightest problems and who tend, nonetheless, to get a lion's share of any assistance. A more discerning measure than unemployment is required to focus attention on those who have the most severe employment problems.

Even if the above assumptions and beliefs are rejected, it is difficult to deny the evidence that low earnings, unemployment, discouragement, and restricted hours of employment are critical and widespread problems—affecting ten million labor force participants according to the EEI estimates. To mount efforts to alleviate these pathologies, or even to decide to do nothing, requires more information about the nature and dimensions of employment problems. The EEI index is only one tentative approach, but it demonstrates the feasibility of an inadequacy measure, the need for such a "new" social indicator, and the severity of the problems to which it is addressed.

# Appendix

CHARACTERISTICS OF SUBEMPLOYED AND PERSONS WITH INADEQUATE EMPLOYMENT
AND EARNINGS BY SEX, COLOR, FAMILY STATUS AND RESIDENCE

1968

| ALL PERSONS | TOTAL | | | FAMILY HEADS (000) | WIVES (000) | OTHER RELATIVES (000) | UNRELATED INDIVIDUALS (000) |
|---|---|---|---|---|---|---|---|
| | NUMBER (000) | AVERAGE HOUSEHOLD INCOME | PERCENT POOR | | | | |
| TOTAL | 131,786 | $ 7,678 | 12.4 | 48,994 | 43,444 | 26,236 | 13,113 |
| IN LABOR FORCE | 77,941 | 8,784 | 7.5 | 40,462 | 16,799 | 13,381 | 7,300 |
| SUBEMPLOYED | 9,907 | 4,997 | 40.5 | 5,772 | 1,363 | 1,271 | 1,501 |
| UNEMPLOYED | 2,384 | 7,152 | 19.4 | 800 | 613 | 757 | 213 |
| DISCOURAGED | 481 | 5,964 | 31.5 | 73 | 209 | 120 | 79 |
| LOW-PD FULL-EMP HEAD | 2,802 | 4,052 | 54.4 | 2,458 | --- | --- | 345 |
| OTHER LOW-EARN HEAD | 2,849 | 3,240 | 59.7 | 2,067 | --- | --- | 781 |
| EMP PART-TIME INVOL | 1,391 | 7,347 | 12.6 | 373 | 541 | 394 | 83 |
| PERCENT SUBEMPLOYED | 12.7% | --- | --- | 14.3% | 8.1% | 9.5% | 20.6% |
| | | | | | | | |
| INADEQUATE EMP/EARN | 8,099 | 3,530 | 49.5 | 5,032 | 925 | 796 | 1,346 |
| UNEMPLOYED | 1,589 | 4,608 | 29.1 | 607 | 378 | 455 | 148 |
| DISCOURAGED | 383 | 3,828 | 39.6 | 59 | 170 | 80 | 74 |
| LOW-PD FULL-EMP HEAD | 2,536 | 3,284 | 60.1 | 2,202 | --- | --- | 334 |
| OTHER LOW-EARN HEAD | 2,660 | 2,697 | 63.9 | 1,904 | --- | --- | 756 |
| EMP PART-TIME INVOL | 932 | 5,201 | 18.9 | 260 | 377 | 261 | 34 |
| EEI INDEX | 10.4% | --- | --- | 12.4% | 5.5% | 6.0% | 18.4% |

1972

| NUMBER (000) | TOTAL AVERAGE HOUSEHOLD INCOME | PERCENT POOR | FAMILY HEADS (000) | WIVES (000) | OTHER RELATIVES (000) | UNRELATED INDIVIDUALS (000) |
|---|---|---|---|---|---|---|
| 3,131 | $ 9,972 | 11.3 | 52,371 | 45,962 | 28,603 | 16,195 |
| 6,122 | 11,528 | 6.9 | 42,478 | 19,320 | 15,431 | 8,894 |
| 2,869 | 7,340 | 32.9 | 6,834 | 1,921 | 2,171 | 1,942 |
| 4,235 | 9,834 | 16.9 | 1,434 | 998 | 1,350 | 454 |
| 724 | 7,629 | 32.5 | 144 | 290 | 249 | 41 |
| 2,335 | 5,452 | 51.9 | 2,092 | --- | --- | 243 |
| 3,682 | 4,320 | 52.4 | 2,653 | --- | --- | 1,029 |
| 1,894 | 10,656 | 7.3 | 513 | 633 | 572 | 175 |
| 14.9% | --- | --- | 16.1% | 9.9% | 14.1% | 21.8% |
| 9,942 | 4,780 | 42.6 | 5,839 | 1,217 | 1,200 | 1,686 |
| 2,731 | 6,070 | 26.3 | 1,057 | 649 | 709 | 316 |
| 542 | 4,743 | 43.4 | 139 | 177 | 191 | 36 |
| 2,078 | 4,245 | 58.3 | 1,841 | --- | --- | 237 |
| 3,478 | 3,712 | 55.5 | 2,472 | --- | --- | 1,006 |
| 1,113 | 6,642 | 12.5 | 330 | 391 | 301 | 92 |
| 11.5% | --- | --- | 13.7% | 6.3% | 7.8% | 19.0% |

1968

**ALL MALE**

| | TOTAL | | | | | | |
| | NUMBER (000) | AVERAGE HOUSEHOLD INCOME | PERCENT POOR | FAMILY HEADS (000) | WIVES (000) | OTHER RELATIVES (000) | UNRELATED INDIVIDUA (000) |
|---|---|---|---|---|---|---|---|
| TOTAL | 61,697 | $ 8,708 | 9.8 | 43,628 | | 13,223 | 4,846 |
| IN LABOR FORCE | 48,808 | 9,515 | 6.5 | 37,679 | | 7,828 | 3,300 |
| SUBEMPLOYED | 5,971 | 5,057 | 41.2 | 4,577 | | 820 | 574 |
| UNEMPLOYED | 1,269 | 7,293 | 18.8 | 670 | | 501 | 99 |
| DISCOURAGED | 126 | 5,295 | 32.1 | 24 | | 59 | 44 |
| LOW-PD FULL-EMP HEAD | 2,245 | 4,235 | 53.7 | 2,091 | | --- | 154 |
| OTHER LOW-EARN HEAD | 1,678 | 3,766 | 54.7 | 1,446 | | --- | 232 |
| EMP PART-TIME INVOL | 653 | 7,455 | 8.9 | 346 | | 261 | 46 |
| PERCENT SUBEMPLOYED | 12.2% | --- | --- | 12.1% | | 10.5% | 17.4% |
| INADEQUATE EMP/EARN | 4,925 | 3,674 | 49.9 | 3,917 | | 518 | 490 |
| UNEMPLOYED | 835 | 4,705 | 28.5 | 484 | | 300 | 51 |
| DISCOURAGED | 99 | 3,217 | 46.1 | 15 | | 40 | 44 |
| LOW-PD FULL-EMP HEAD | 2,020 | 3,434 | 59.6 | 1,868 | | --- | 152 |
| OTHER LOW-EARN HEAD | 1,542 | 3,091 | 59.6 | 1,315 | | --- | 226 |
| EMP PART-TIME INVOL | 430 | 5,348 | 13.5 | 234 | | 179 | 17 |
| EEI INDEX | 10.1% | --- | --- | 10.4% | | 6.6% | 14.8% |

1968

**ALL FEMALE**

| | TOTAL | | | | | | |
| | NUMBER (000) | AVERAGE HOUSEHOLD INCOME | PERCENT POOR | FAMILY HEADS (000) | WIVES (000) | OTHER RELATIVES (000) | UNRELATED INDIVIDUAL (000) |
|---|---|---|---|---|---|---|---|
| TOTAL | 70,089 | $ 7,937 | 14.6 | 5,366 | 43,444 | 13,012 | 8,267 |
| IN LABOR FORCE | 29,133 | 8,978 | 9.0 | 2,782 | 16,799 | 5,552 | 3,999 |
| SUBEMPLOYED | 3,936 | 5,013 | 39.4 | 1,195 | 1,363 | 451 | 927 |
| UNEMPLOYED | 1,114 | 6,970 | 20.1 | 131 | 613 | 257 | 114 |
| DISCOURAGED | 355 | 6,192 | 31.2 | 49 | 209 | 61 | 36 |
| LOW-PD FULL-EMP HEAD | 558 | 3,313 | 57.2 | 367 | --- | --- | 191 |
| OTHER LOW-EARN HEAD | 1,171 | 2,488 | 66.8 | 621 | --- | --- | 550 |
| EMP PART-TIME INVOL | 738 | 7,275 | 16.0 | 27 | 541 | 133 | 37 |
| PERCENT SUBEMPLOYED | 13.5% | --- | --- | 43.0% | 8.1% | 8.1% | 23.2% |
| INADEQUATE EMP/EARN | 3,174 | 3,385 | 49.9 | 1,114 | 925 | 278 | 857 |
| UNEMPLOYED | 753 | 4,546 | 29.7 | 123 | 378 | 155 | 97 |
| DISCOURAGED | 284 | 4,036 | 39.0 | 44 | 170 | 40 | 30 |
| LOW-PD FULL-EMP HEAD | 516 | 2,699 | 61.8 | 333 | --- | --- | 183 |
| OTHER LOW-EARN HEAD | 1,119 | 2,155 | 69.9 | 588 | --- | --- | 530 |
| EMP PART-TIME INVOL | 502 | 5,086 | 23.5 | 26 | 377 | 82 | 17 |
| EEI INDEX | 10.9% | --- | --- | 40.1% | 5.5% | 5.0% | 21.4% |

1972

| NUMBER (000) | TOTAL AVERAGE HOUSEHOLD INCOME | PERCENT POOR | FAMILY HEADS (000) | WIVES (000) | OTHER RELATIVES (000) | UNRELATED INDIVIDUALS (000) |
|---|---|---|---|---|---|---|
| 7,222 | $ 11,424 | 8.8 | 46,117 | | 14,767 | 6,338 |
| 2,643 | 12,545 | 6.1 | 39,097 | | 9,166 | 4,380 |
| 7,709 | 7,550 | 32.5 | 5,369 | | 1,409 | 931 |
| 2, | 10,310 | 15.2 | 1,221 | | 910 | 295 |
| 187 | 6,540 | 37.1 | 53 | | 123 | 12 |
| 1,872 | 5,602 | 51.6 | 1,768 | | --- | 103 |
| 2,264 | 5,044 | 46.7 | 1,862 | | --- | 402 |
| 960 | 11,285 | 4.9 | 465 | | 376 | 119 |
| 14.6% | --- | --- | 13.7% | | 15.4% | 21.3% |
| 5,948 | 4,963 | 42.2 | 4,454 | | 737 | 757 |
| 1,486 | 6,166 | 24.9 | 851 | | 447 | 188 |
| 165 | 5,045 | 42.1 | 48 | | 105 | 12 |
| 1,660 | 4,351 | 58.1 | 1,557 | | --- | 103 |
| 2,110 | 4,274 | 50.0 | 1,714 | | --- | |
| 527 | 6,807 | 9.0 | 283 | | 185 | 59 |
| 11.3% | --- | --- | 11.4% | | 8.0% | 17.3% |

1972

| NUMBER (000) | TOTAL AVERAGE HOUSEHOLD INCOME | PERCENT POOR | FAMILY HEADS (000) | WIVES (000) | OTHER RELATIVES (000) | UNRELATED INDIVIDUALS (000) |
|---|---|---|---|---|---|---|
| 75,909 | $ 10,382 | 13.6 | 6,254 | 45,962 | 13,837 | 9,856 |
| 33,479 | 11,850 | 8.1 | 3,381 | 19,320 | 6,265 | 4,513 |
| 5,160 | 7,059 | 33.4 | 1,465 | 1,921 | 763 | 1,011 |
| 1,809 | 9,171 | 19.2 | 213 | 998 | 440 | 159 |
| 537 | 8,010 | 30.9 | 91 | 290 | 127 | 28 |
| 463 | 4,849 | 53.4 | 323 | --- | --- | 140 |
| 1,418 | 3,168 | 61.5 | 791 | --- | --- | 627 |
| 934 | 10,051 | 9.8 | 48 | 633 | 197 | 56 |
| 15.4% | --- | --- | 43.3% | 9.9% | 12.2% | 22.4% |
| 3,994 | 4,595 | 43.2 | 1,385 | 217 | 463 | 929 |
| 1,244 | 5,961 | 27.9 | 206 | 649 | 261 | 129 |
| 378 | 4,735 | 43.9 | 91 | 177 | 86 | 24 |
| 418 | 3,826 | 59.2 | 284 | --- | --- | 133 |
| 1,368 | 2,843 | 63.7 | 758 | --- | --- | 610 |
| 586 | 6,491 | 15.6 | 46 | 391 | 115 | 33 |
| 11.9% | --- | --- | 41.0% | 6.3% | 7.4% | 20.6% |

1968

## ALL WHITE

| | NUMBER (000) | TOTAL AVERAGE HOUSEHOLD INCOME | PERCENT POOR | FAMILY HEADS (000) | WIVES (000) | OTHER RELATIVES (000) | UNRELATED INDIVIDUALS (000) |
|---|---|---|---|---|---|---|---|
| TOTAL | 117,665 | $ 8,001 | 10.2 | 44,005 | 39,959 | 22,404 | 11,296 |
| IN LABOR FORCE | 69,186 | 9,136 | 5.6 | 36,616 | 15,022 | 11,418 | 6,130 |
| SUBEMPLOYED | 7,392 | 5,297 | 36.2 | 4,289 | 1,100 | 910 | 1,094 |
| UNEMPLOYED | 1,843 | 7,661 | 14.5 | 629 | 512 | 543 | 159 |
| DISCOURAGED | 348 | 6,554 | 26.5 | 38 | 170 | 95 | 45 |
| LOW-PD FULL-EMP HEAD | 1,981 | 3,977 | 53.8 | 1,717 | --- | --- | 265 |
| OTHER LOW-EARN HEAD | 2,141 | 3,407 | 54.6 | 1,579 | --- | --- | 563 |
| EMP PART-TIME INVOL | 1,079 | 7,799 | 7.7 | 326 | 418 | 273 | 63 |
| PERCENT SUBEMPLOYED | 10.7% | --- | --- | 11.7% | 7.3% | 8.0% | 17.8% |
| | | | | | | | |
| INADEQUATE EMP/EARN | 5,843 | 3,620 | 45.8 | 3,657 | 703 | 517 | 966 |
| UNEMPLOYED | 1,150 | 4,858 | 23.2 | 455 | 294 | 294 | 106 |
| DISCOURAGED | 269 | 4,189 | 34.3 | 24 | 134 | 65 | 45 |
| LOW-PD FULL-EMP HEAD | 1,774 | 3,126 | 60.1 | 1,518 | --- | --- | 256 |
| OTHER LOW-EARN HEAD | 1,977 | 2,807 | 59.1 | 1,440 | --- | --- | 538 |
| EMP PART-TIME INVOL | 674 | 5,451 | 12.4 | 220 | 274 | 158 | 22 |
| EEI INDEX | 8.4% | --- | --- | 10.0% | 4.7% | 4.5% | 15.8% |

1968

## ALL BLACK

| | NUMBER (000) | TOTAL AVERAGE HOUSEHOLD INCOME | PERCENT POOR | FAMILY HEADS (000) | WIVES (000) | OTHER RELATIVES (000) | UNRELATED INDIVIDUALS (000) |
|---|---|---|---|---|---|---|---|
| TOTAL | 12,857 | $ 4,876 | 32.2 | 4,568 | 3,108 | 3,519 | 1,663 |
| IN LABOR FORCE | 7,992 | 5,633 | 23.2 | 3,493 | 1,608 | 1,823 | 1,067 |
| SUBEMPLOYED | 2,388 | 3,965 | 54.0 | 1,414 | 242 | 348 | 385 |
| UNEMPLOYED | 514 | 5,233 | 36.2 | 158 | 97 | 206 | 53 |
| DISCOURAGED | 125 | 3,894 | 47.4 | 35 | 35 | 20 | 35 |
| LOW-PD FULL-EMP HEAD | 786 | 4,154 | 56.5 | 709 | --- | --- | 77 |
| OTHER LOW-EARN HEAD | 667 | 2,668 | 76.0 | 465 | --- | --- | 202 |
| EMP PART-TIME INVOL | 297 | 5,427 | 31.2 | 48 | 110 | 121 | 18 |
| PERCENT SUBEMPLOYED | 29.9% | --- | --- | 40.5% | 15.0% | 19.1% | 36.1% |
| | | | | | | | |
| INADEQUATE EMP/EARN | 2,170 | 3,280 | 59.4 | 1,324 | 213 | 274 | 359 |
| UNEMPLOYED | 420 | 3,930 | 44.3 | 143 | 80 | 156 | 41 |
| DISCOURAGED | 114 | 2,953 | 51.9 | 35 | 35 | 15 | 29 |
| LOW-PD FULL-EMP HEAD | 735 | 3,630 | 60.4 | 659 | --- | --- | 76 |
| OTHER LOW-EARN HEAD | 648 | 2,380 | 78.7 | 446 | --- | --- | 202 |
| EMP PART-TIME INVOL | 252 | 4,455 | 36.7 | 40 | 98 | 103 | 12 |
| EEI INDEX | 27.2% | --- | --- | 37.9% | 13.2% | 15.0% | 33.7% |

1972

| UMBER (000) | TOTAL AVERAGE HOUSEHOLD INCOME | PERCENT POOR | FAMILY HEADS (000) | WIVES (000) | OTHER RELATIVES (000) | UNRELATED INDIVIDUALS (000) |
|---|---|---|---|---|---|---|
| 7,099 | $ 10,373 | 9.4 | 46,748 | 42,210 | 24,036 | 14,105 |
| 6,489 | 11,937 | 5.5 | 38,344 | 17,335 | 13,140 | 7,671 |
| 0,177 | 7,729 | 29.4 | 5,373 | 1,651 | 1,594 | 1,559 |
| 3,410 | 10,462 | 13.6 | 1,188 | 842 | 1,031 | 349 |
| 488 | 8,737 | 18.7 | 88 | 251 | 118 | 31 |
| 1,764 | 5,163 | 52.0 | 1,567 | --- | --- | 197 |
| 2,917 | 4,451 | 49.3 | 2,075 | --- | --- | 842 |
| 1,598 | 11,218 | 5.0 | 455 | 558 | 445 | 140 |
| 13.3% | --- | --- | 14.0% | 9.5% | 12.1% | 20.3% |
| 7,614 | 4,859 | 39.3 | 4,520 | 995 | 758 | 1,341 |
| 2,084 | 6,320 | 22.3 | 848 | 528 | 473 | 235 |
| 331 | 5,298 | 27.6 | 83 | 143 | 79 | 26 |
| 1,569 | 3,976 | 58.4 | 1,377 | --- | --- | 192 |
| 2,749 | 3,808 | 52.4 | 1,928 | --- | --- | 821 |
| 882 | 6,807 | 9.0 | 285 | 324 | 206 | 68 |
| 10.0% | --- | --- | 11.8% | 5.7% | 5.8% | 17.5% |

1972

| UMBER (000) | TOTAL AVERAGE HOUSEHOLD INCOME | PERCENT POOR | FAMILY HEADS (000) | WIVES (000) | OTHER RELATIVES (000) | UNRELATED INDIVIDUALS (000) |
|---|---|---|---|---|---|---|
| 4,442 | $ 6,557 | 27.9 | 5,121 | 3,272 | 4,171 | 1,878 |
| 8,671 | 7,811 | 18.2 | 3,704 | 1,764 | 2,108 | 1,095 |
| 2,500 | 5,626 | 46.6 | 1,351 | 245 | 550 | 354 |
| 767 | 6,861 | 32.0 | 226 | 140 | 304 | 97 |
| 204 | 5,321 | 59.3 | 38 | 34 | 122 | 10 |
| 542 | 6,297 | 51.9 | 496 | --- | --- | 45 |
| 708 | 3,786 | 64.7 | 534 | --- | --- | 174 |
| 280 | 7,261 | 21.3 | 56 | 71 | 124 | 28 |
| 28.8% | --- | --- | 36.5% | 13.9% | 26.1% | 32.4% |
| 2,185 | 4,501 | 53.4 | 1,226 | 206 | 426 | 327 |
| 613 | 5,208 | 40.1 | 199 | 112 | 225 | 77 |
| 185 | 4,170 | 65.7 | 38 | 29 | 108 | 10 |
| 484 | 5,066 | 58.1 | 440 | --- | --- | 43 |
| 679 | 3,342 | 67.5 | 505 | --- | --- | 174 |
| 224 | 5,923 | 26.5 | 43 | 65 | 93 | 23 |
| 25.2% | --- | --- | 33.1% | 11.7% | 20.2% | 29.9% |

1968

| WHITE MALE | | TOTAL | | | | | |
|---|---|---|---|---|---|---|---|
| | | AVERAGE | | FAMILY | | OTHER | UNRELATED |
| | NUMBER | HOUSEHOLD | PERCENT | HEADS | WIVES | RELATIVES | INDIVIDUAL |
| | (000) | INCOME | POOR | (000) | (000) | (000) | (000) |
| TOTAL | 55,258 | $ 9,010 | 7.9 | 39,985 | | 11,321 | 3,952 |
| IN LABOR FORCE | 43,839 | 9,823 | 5.0 | 34,535 | | 6,648 | 2,656 |
| SUBEMPLOYED | 4,539 | 5,253 | 38.1 | 3,554 | | 594 | 391 |
| UNEMPLOYED | 998 | 7,726 | 14.1 | 560 | | 363 | 75 |
| DISCOURAGED | 88 | 6,179 | 28.3 | 19 | | 43 | 26 |
| LOW-PD FULL-EMP HEAD | 1,640 | 4,095 | 53.9 | 1,519 | | ---- | 120 |
| OTHER LOW-EARN HEAD | 1,287 | 3,943 | 50.6 | 1,151 | | ---- | 136 |
| EMP PART-TIME INVOL | 526 | 7,761 | 5.3 | 305 | | 187 | 34 |
| PERCENT SUBEMPLOYED | 10.4% | ---- | ---- | 10.3% | | 8.9% | 14.7% |
| INADEQUATE EMP/EARN | 3,662 | 3,710 | 47.2 | 2,992 | | 345 | 325 |
| UNEMPLOYED | 625 | 4,930 | 22.5 | 393 | | 195 | 38 |
| DISCOURAGED | 65 | 3,877 | 38.4 | 10 | | 30 | 26 |
| LOW-PD FULL-EMP HEAD | 1,466 | 3,243 | 60.2 | 1,348 | | ---- | 118 |
| OTHER LOW-EARN HEAD | 1,171 | 3,217 | 55.6 | 1,041 | | ---- | 131 |
| EMP PART-TIME INVOL | 334 | 5,491 | 8.4 | 200 | | 120 | 13 |
| EEI INDEX | 8.4% | ---- | ---- | 8.7% | | 5.2% | 12.2% |

1968

| WHITE FEMALE | | TOTAL | | | | | |
|---|---|---|---|---|---|---|---|
| | | AVERAGE | | FAMILY | | OTHER | UNRELATE |
| | NUMBER | HOUSEHOLD | PERCENT | HEADS | WIVES | RELATIVES | INDIVIDUA |
| | (000) | INCOME | POOR | (000) | (000) | (000) | (000) |
| TOTAL | 62,406 | $ 8,235 | 12.2 | 4,020 | 39,959 | 11,083 | 7,344 |
| IN LABOR FORCE | 25,347 | 9,360 | 6.7 | 2,081 | 15,022 | 4,770 | 3,474 |
| SUBEMPLOYED | 2,853 | 5,475 | 33.3 | 735 | 1,100 | 316 | 703 |
| UNEMPLOYED | 844 | 7,603 | 15.0 | 70 | 512 | 179 | 84 |
| DISCOURAGED | 260 | 6,679 | 25.9 | 19 | 170 | 51 | 19 |
| LOW-PD FULL-EMP HEAD | 342 | 3,412 | 53.6 | 197 | ---- | ---- | 144 |
| OTHER LOW-EARN HEAD | 854 | 2,600 | 60.6 | 428 | ---- | ---- | 427 |
| EMP PART-TIME INVOL | 553 | 7,857 | 10.0 | 21 | 418 | 85 | 29 |
| PERCENT SUBEMPLOYED | 11.3% | ---- | ---- | 35.3% | 7.3% | 6.6% | 20.2% |
| INADEQUATE EMP/EARN | 2,181 | 3,528 | 43.6 | 665 | 703 | 172 | 641 |
| UNEMPLOYED | 524 | 4,849 | 24.2 | 63 | 294 | 99 | 69 |
| DISCOURAGED | 204 | 4,290 | 33.0 | 14 | 134 | 36 | 19 |
| LOW-PD FULL-EMP HEAD | 307 | 2,571 | 59.6 | 169 | ---- | ---- | 138 |
| OTHER LOW-EARN HEAD | 806 | 2,212 | 64.2 | 399 | ---- | ---- | 407 |
| EMP PART-TIME INVOL | 340 | 5,401 | 16.3 | 20 | 274 | 38 | 9 |
| EEI INDEX | 8.6% | ---- | ---- | 32.0% | 4.7% | 3.6% | 18.5% |

104

1972

| NUMBER (000) | TOTAL AVERAGE HOUSEHOLD INCOME | PERCENT POOR | FAMILY HEADS (000) | WIVES (000) | OTHER RELATIVES (000) | UNRELATED INDIVIDUALS (000) |
|---|---|---|---|---|---|---|
| ,972 | $ 11,773 | 7.3 | 42,225 | | 12,434 | 5,313 |
| ,337 | 12,881 | 5.1 | 35,842 | | 7,779 | 3,716 |
| ,212 | 7,799 | 30.7 | 4,413 | | 1,061 | 738 |
| ,002 | 10,848 | 12.8 | 1,063 | | 716 | 223 |
| 94 | 6,759 | 20.5 | 38 | | 49 | 8 |
| ,457 | 5,261 | 52.1 | 1,372 | | --- | 85 |
| ,862 | 5,096 | 45.0 | 1,530 | | --- | 332 |
| 796 | 11,904 | 4.0 | 410 | | 296 | 91 |
| 13.1% | --- | --- | 12.3% | | 13.6% | 19.9% |
| ,702 | 4,967 | 40.5 | 3,621 | | 485 | 597 |
| ,171 | 6,350 | 21.9 | 725 | | 310 | 137 |
| 83 | 6,023 | 23.2 | 33 | | 43 | 8 |
| ,295 | 4,053 | 58.6 | 1,210 | | --- | 85 |
| ,742 | 4,339 | 48.1 | 1,414 | | --- | 328 |
| 411 | 7,003 | 7.8 | 239 | | 132 | 39 |
| 9.9% | --- | --- | 10.1% | | 6.2% | 16.1% |

1972

| NUMBER (000) | TOTAL AVERAGE HOUSEHOLD INCOME | PERCENT POOR | FAMILY HEADS (000) | WIVES (000) | OTHER RELATIVES (000) | UNRELATED INDIVIDUALS (000) |
|---|---|---|---|---|---|---|
| 7,127 | $ 10,758 | 11.2 | 4,523 | 42,210 | 11,602 | 8,792 |
| 9,152 | 12,285 | 6.2 | 2,502 | 17,335 | 5,361 | 3,955 |
| 3,965 | 7,667 | 27.4 | 960 | 1,651 | 533 | 821 |
| 1,408 | 9,857 | 14.7 | 125 | 842 | 315 | 127 |
| 393 | 9,233 | 18.2 | 50 | 251 | 69 | 23 |
| 306 | 4,699 | 51.4 | 195 | --- | --- | 112 |
| 1,055 | 3,315 | 57.0 | 545 | --- | --- | 510 |
| 802 | 10,594 | 5.9 | 45 | 558 | 149 | 50 |
| 13.6% | --- | --- | 38.4% | 9.5% | 9.9% | 20.8% |
| 2,912 | 4,780 | 37.2 | 899 | 995 | 273 | 745 |
| 913 | 6,272 | 22.7 | 123 | 528 | 164 | 98 |
| 247 | 5,202 | 29.0 | 50 | 143 | 36 | 18 |
| 274 | 3,611 | 57.5 | 167 | --- | --- | 107 |
| 1,007 | 2,890 | 59.7 | 514 | --- | --- | 493 |
| 471 | 6,646 | 10.0 | 45 | 324 | 73 | 29 |
| 10.0% | --- | --- | 35.9% | 5.7% | 5.1% | 18.8% |

1968

**BLACK MALE**

| | NUMBER (000) | TOTAL AVERAGE HOUSEHOLD INCOME | PERCENT POOR | FAMILY HEADS (000) | WIVES (000) | OTHER RELATIVES (000) | UNRELATED INDIVIDUALS (000) |
|---|---|---|---|---|---|---|---|
| TOTAL | 5,807 | $ 5,767 | 27.1 | 3,274 | | 1,748 | 786 |
| IN LABOR FORCE | 4,486 | 6,401 | 21.1 | 2,813 | | 1,105 | 568 |
| SUBEMPLOYED | 1,345 | 4,365 | 51.8 | 962 | | 216 | 167 |
| UNEMPLOYED | 254 | 5,528 | 36.2 | 98 | | 132 | 24 |
| DISCOURAGED | 34 | 1,818 | 46.4 | 5 | | 11 | 18 |
| LOW-PD FULL-EMP HEAD | 571 | 4,543 | 54.0 | 540 | | --- | 31 |
| OTHER LOW-EARN HEAD | 361 | 3,146 | 69.6 | 277 | | --- | 84 |
| EMP PART-TIME INVOL | 125 | 5,982 | 24.0 | 42 | | 74 | 10 |
| PERCENT SUBEMPLOYED | 30.0% | --- | --- | 34.2% | | 19.6% | 29.4% |
| | | | | | | | |
| INADEQUATE EMP/EARN | 1,200 | 3,573 | 58.1 | 880 | | 169 | 150 |
| UNEMPLOYED | 198 | 4,021 | 46.3 | 84 | | 100 | 14 |
| DISCOURAGED | 34 | 1,818 | 46.4 | 5 | | 11 | 18 |
| LOW-PD FULL-EMP HEAD | 527 | 3,924 | 58.6 | 496 | | --- | 31 |
| OTHER LOW-EARN HEAD | 345 | 2,691 | 72.8 | 261 | | --- | 84 |
| EMP PART-TIME INVOL | 96 | 4,767 | 31.3 | 34 | | 58 | 4 |
| EEI INDEX | 26.7% | --- | --- | 31.3% | | 15.3% | 26.5% |

1968

**BLACK FEMALE**

| | NUMBER (000) | TOTAL AVERAGE HOUSEHOLD INCOME | PERCENT POOR | FAMILY HEADS (000) | WIVES (000) | OTHER RELATIVES (000) | UNRELATED INDIVIDUALS (000) |
|---|---|---|---|---|---|---|---|
| TOTAL | 7,050 | $ 5,099 | 36.4 | 1,294 | 3,108 | 1,771 | 877 |
| IN LABOR FORCE | 3,506 | 6,072 | 25.8 | 680 | 1,608 | 718 | 499 |
| SUBEMPLOYED | 1,043 | 3,618 | 56.7 | 452 | 242 | 132 | 218 |
| UNEMPLOYED | 260 | 4,920 | 36.3 | 60 | 97 | 74 | 29 |
| DISCOURAGED | 92 | 4,596 | 47.8 | 30 | 35 | 10 | 17 |
| LOW-PD FULL-EMP HEAD | 215 | 3,121 | 63.1 | 169 | --- | --- | 46 |
| OTHER LOW-EARN HEAD | 305 | 2,103 | 83.6 | 188 | --- | --- | 118 |
| EMP PART-TIME INVOL | 171 | 5,100 | 36.4 | 6 | 110 | 47 | 8 |
| PERCENT SUBEMPLOYED | 29.8% | --- | --- | 66.5% | 15.0% | 18.3% | 43.6% |
| | | | | | | | |
| INADEQUATE EMP/EARN | 970 | 3,056 | 61.0 | 444 | 213 | 104 | 209 |
| UNEMPLOYED | 222 | 3,856 | 42.5 | 59 | 80 | 55 | 28 |
| DISCOURAGED | 81 | 3,392 | 54.2 | 30 | 35 | 5 | 11 |
| LOW-PD FULL-EMP HEAD | 209 | 2,887 | 65.0 | 164 | --- | --- | 45 |
| OTHER LOW-EARN HEAD | 303 | 2,026 | 84.3 | 185 | --- | --- | 118 |
| EMP PART-TIME INVOL | 156 | 4,329 | 40.0 | 6 | 98 | 44 | 8 |
| EEI INDEX | 27.7% | --- | --- | 65.2% | 13.2% | 14.6% | 41.9% |

1972

| NUMBER (000) | TOTAL AVERAGE HOUSEHOLD INCOME | PERCENT POOR | FAMILY HEADS (000) | WIVES (000) | OTHER RELATIVES (000) | UNRELATED INDIVIDUALS (000) |
|---|---|---|---|---|---|---|
| 6,487 | $ 7,952 | 21.7 | 3,464 | | 2,137 | 887 |
| 4,749 | 8,917 | 15.5 | 2,881 | | 1,278 | 589 |
| 1,389 | 6,296 | 41.2 | 884 | | 328 | 177 |
| 387 | 7,294 | 27.6 | 139 | | 182 | 66 |
| 88 | 5,567 | 56.8 | 15 | | 69 | 4 |
| 391 | 6,724 | 49.9 | 373 | | --- | 18 |
| 367 | 4,754 | 55.8 | 303 | | --- | 64 |
| 155 | 7,936 | 10.0 | 53 | | 77 | 24 |
| 29.2% | --- | --- | 30.7% | | 25.7% | 30.0% |
| | | | | | | |
| 1,174 | 4,953 | 48.8 | 777 | | 244 | 153 |
| 293 | 5,475 | 36.4 | 116 | | 129 | 48 |
| 81 | 3,725 | 61.5 | 15 | | 62 | 4 |
| 347 | 5,393 | 56.3 | 328 | | --- | 18 |
| 340 | 3,971 | 60.3 | 276 | | --- | 64 |
| 113 | 5,988 | 13.8 | 42 | | 52 | 18 |
| 24.7% | --- | --- | 27.0% | | 19.1% | 25.9% |

1972

| NUMBER (000) | TOTAL AVERAGE HOUSEHOLD INCOME | PERCENT POOR | FAMILY HEADS (000) | WIVES (000) | OTHER RELATIVES (000) | UNRELATED INDIVIDUALS (000) |
|---|---|---|---|---|---|---|
| 7,955 | $ 6,853 | 32.9 | 1,657 | 3,272 | 2,034 | 991 |
| 3,922 | 8,402 | 21.6 | 822 | 1,764 | 830 | 506 |
| 1,112 | 4,845 | 53.4 | 467 | 245 | 222 | 177 |
| 379 | 6,471 | 36.6 | 88 | 140 | 122 | 30 |
| 116 | 5,164 | 61.3 | 23 | 34 | 53 | 6 |
| 150 | 5,185 | 57.2 | 123 | --- | --- | 27 |
| 341 | 2,742 | 74.4 | 231 | --- | --- | 110 |
| 125 | 6,545 | 35.2 | 3 | 71 | 47 | 4 |
| 28.3% | --- | --- | 56.8% | 13.9% | 26.8% | 35.1% |
| | | | | | | |
| 1,011 | 4,068 | 58.7 | 448 | 206 | 183 | 174 |
| 320 | 4,990 | 43.4 | 83 | 112 | 96 | 29 |
| 103 | 4,459 | 68.9 | 23 | 29 | 46 | 6 |
| 137 | 4,242 | 62.6 | 112 | --- | --- | 25 |
| 339 | 2,711 | 74.7 | 229 | --- | --- | 110 |
| 112 | 5,785 | 39.4 | 1 | 65 | 41 | 4 |
| 25.8% | --- | --- | 54.5% | 11.7% | 22.0% | 34.4% |

107

1968

**ALL IN SMSA**

| | NUMBER (000) | TOTAL AVERAGE HOUSEHOLD INCOME | PERCENT POOR | FAMILY HEADS (000) | WIVES (000) | OTHER RELATIVES (000) | UNRELATED INDIVIDUALS (000) |
|---|---|---|---|---|---|---|---|
| TOTAL | 85,962 | $ 8,300 | 9.6 | 31,667 | 27,798 | 17,238 | 9,259 |
| IN LABOR FORCE | 51,253 | 9,458 | 5.3 | 26,388 | 10,485 | 8,955 | 5,425 |
| SUBEMPLOYED | 5,462 | 5,473 | 36.1 | 2,928 | 758 | 756 | 1,020 |
| UNEMPLOYED | 1,520 | 7,648 | 16.0 | 491 | 381 | 487 | 161 |
| DISCOURAGED | 273 | 7,612 | 19.9 | 29 | 110 | 76 | 59 |
| LOW-PD FULL-EMP HEAD | 1,304 | 4,527 | 51.2 | 1,083 | --- | --- | 220 |
| OTHER LOW-EARN HEAD | 1,636 | 3,367 | 58.0 | 1,115 | --- | --- | 521 |
| EMP PART-TIME INVOL | 730 | 7,970 | 8.0 | 211 | 267 | 193 | 58 |
| PERCENT SUBEMPLOYED | 10.7% | --- | --- | 11.1% | 7.2% | 8.4% | 18.8% |
| | | | | | | | |
| INADEQUATE EMP/EARN | 4,507 | 3,903 | 43.7 | 2,602 | 522 | 458 | 924 |
| UNEMPLOYED | 1,049 | 4,969 | 23.1 | 394 | 243 | 293 | 119 |
| DISCOURAGED | 199 | 4,820 | 27.3 | 19 | 85 | 42 | 53 |
| LOW-PD FULL-EMP HEAD | 1,193 | 3,734 | 56.0 | 980 | --- | --- | 212 |
| OTHER LOW-EARN HEAD | 1,557 | 2,841 | 60.9 | 1,046 | --- | --- | 512 |
| EMP PART-TIME INVOL | 508 | 5,885 | 11.4 | 163 | 195 | 123 | 27 |
| EEI INDEX | 8.8% | --- | --- | 9.9% | 5.0% | 5.1% | 17.0% |

1968

**ALL NOT IN SMSA**

| | NUMBER (000) | TOTAL AVERAGE HOUSEHOLD INCOME | PERCENT POOR | FAMILY HEADS (000) | WIVES (000) | OTHER RELATIVES (000) | UNRELATED INDIVIDUALS (000) |
|---|---|---|---|---|---|---|---|
| TOTAL | 45,824 | $ 6,517 | 17.5 | 17,327 | 15,646 | 8,997 | 3,854 |
| IN LABOR FORCE | 26,688 | 7,470 | 11.5 | 14,074 | 6,314 | 4,425 | 1,874 |
| SUBEMPLOYED | 4,446 | 4,409 | 45.9 | 2,844 | 606 | 515 | 481 |
| UNEMPLOYED | 864 | 6,264 | 25.4 | 310 | 232 | 270 | 51 |
| DISCOURAGED | 208 | 3,825 | 46.6 | 45 | 99 | 44 | 21 |
| LOW-PD FULL-EMP HEAD | 1,498 | 3,640 | 57.1 | 1,374 | --- | --- | 124 |
| OTHER LOW-EARN HEAD | 1,213 | 3,071 | 62.0 | 952 | --- | --- | 261 |
| EMP PART-TIME INVOL | 662 | 6,658 | 17.8 | 163 | 274 | 201 | 24 |
| PERCENT SUBEMPLOYED | 16.7% | --- | --- | 20.2% | 9.6% | 11.6% | 25.7% |
| | | | | | | | |
| INADEQUATE EMP/EARN | 3,592 | 3,052 | 56.8 | 2,429 | 403 | 338 | 422 |
| UNEMPLOYED | 539 | 3,904 | 40.6 | 213 | 136 | 162 | 29 |
| DISCOURAGED | 184 | 2,758 | 52.8 | 40 | 85 | 38 | 21 |
| LOW-PD FULL-EMP HEAD | 1,343 | 2,885 | 63.7 | 1,221 | --- | --- | 122 |
| OTHER LOW-EARN HEAD | 1,103 | 2,494 | 68.1 | 858 | --- | --- | 244 |
| EMP PART-TIME INVOL | 423 | 4,370 | 27.8 | 97 | 182 | 138 | 7 |
| EEI INDEX | 13.5% | --- | --- | 17.3% | 6.4% | 7.6% | 22.5% |

1972

| NUMBER (000) | TOTAL AVERAGE HOUSEHOLD INCOME | PERCENT POOR | FAMILY HEADS (000) | WIVES (000) | OTHER RELATIVES (000) | UNRELATED INDIVIDUALS (000) |
|---|---|---|---|---|---|---|
| 98,821 | $ 10,614 | 9.3 | 35,865 | 31,009 | 19,837 | 12,109 |
| 60,179 | 12,198 | 5.5 | 29,434 | 12,970 | 10,748 | 7,028 |
| 8,155 | 7,807 | 30.4 | 4,033 | 1,217 | 1,462 | 1,444 |
| 2,993 | 10,062 | 16.2 | 974 | 676 | 954 | 390 |
| 430 | 8,446 | 33.9 | 95 | 181 | 141 | 12 |
| 1,130 | 5,910 | 50.8 | 970 | --- | --- | 160 |
| 2,375 | 4,376 | 51.4 | 1,631 | --- | --- | 744 |
| 1,227 | 11,311 | 4.5 | 363 | 360 | 366 | 138 |
| 13.6% | --- | --- | 13.7% | 9.4% | 13.6% | 20.5% |
| 6,376 | 5,108 | 38.9 | 3,512 | 791 | 817 | 1,256 |
| 2,018 | 6,307 | 24.0 | 758 | 458 | 519 | 283 |
| 328 | 5,303 | 44.5 | 95 | 107 | 114 | 12 |
| 1,019 | 4,616 | 56.3 | 864 | --- | --- | 155 |
| 2,269 | 3,819 | 53.9 | 1,543 | --- | --- | 727 |
| 742 | 7,061 | 7.5 | 252 | 226 | 185 | 80 |
| 10.6% | --- | --- | 11.9% | 6.1% | 7.6% | 17.9% |

1972

| NUMBER (000) | TOTAL AVERAGE HOUSEHOLD INCOME | PERCENT POOR | FAMILY HEADS (000) | WIVES (000) | OTHER RELATIVES (000) | UNRELATED INDIVIDUALS (000) |
|---|---|---|---|---|---|---|
| 44,309 | $ 8,509 | 15.8 | 16,505 | 14,953 | 8,766 | 4,085 |
| 25,943 | 9,915 | 10.0 | 13,044 | 6,350 | 4,683 | 1,865 |
| 4,714 | 6,524 | 37.2 | 2,801 | 704 | 710 | 498 |
| 1,242 | 9,275 | 18.8 | 460 | 322 | 396 | 64 |
| 294 | 6,398 | 30.4 | 48 | 110 | 108 | 29 |
| 1,205 | 5,025 | 53.0 | 1,122 | --- | --- | 83 |
| 1,306 | 4,223 | 54.1 | 1,022 | --- | --- | 235 |
| 666 | 9,394 | 12.5 | 149 | 273 | 207 | 37 |
| 18.2% | --- | --- | 21.5% | 11.1% | 15.2% | 26.7% |
| 3,566 | 4,186 | 49.1 | 2,327 | 426 | 383 | 430 |
| 713 | 5,394 | 32.8 | 299 | 190 | 190 | 33 |
| 215 | 3,880 | 41.7 | 43 | 70 | 77 | 24 |
| 1,058 | 3,891 | 60.3 | 977 | --- | --- | 82 |
| 1,209 | 3,512 | 58.5 | 930 | --- | --- | 279 |
| 371 | 5,773 | 22.5 | 78 | 165 | 116 | 12 |
| 13.7% | --- | --- | 17.8% | 6.7% | 8.2% | 23.0% |

1968

### IN SMSA - WHITE

| | NUMBER (000) | TOTAL AVERAGE HOUSEHOLD INCOME | PERCENT POOR | FAMILY HEADS (000) | WIVES (000) | OTHER RELATIVES (000) | UNRELATED INDIVIDUALS (000) |
|---|---|---|---|---|---|---|---|
| TOTAL | 76,018 | $ 8,666 | 7.9 | 28,109 | 25,338 | 14,691 | 7,880 |
| IN LABOR FORCE | 44,920 | 9,861 | 3.9 | 23,590 | 9,216 | 7,614 | 4,501 |
| SUBEMPLOYED | 3,933 | 5,829 | 32.6 | 2,077 | 606 | 525 | 725 |
| UNEMPLOYED | 1,137 | 8,253 | 11.5 | 369 | 316 | 335 | 117 |
| DISCOURAGED | 199 | 8,159 | 20.4 | 20 | 92 | 66 | 30 |
| LOW-PD FULL-EMP HEAD | 839 | 4,411 | 52.6 | 669 | --- | --- | 170 |
| OTHER LOW-EARN HEAD | 1,216 | 3,547 | 52.7 | 849 | --- | --- | 367 |
| EMP PART-TIME INVOL | 543 | 8,458 | 5.3 | 170 | 208 | 124 | 41 |
| PERCENT SUBEMPLOYED | 8.8% | --- | --- | 8.8% | 6.6% | 6.9% | 16.1% |
| INADEQUATE EMP/EARN | 3,159 | 4,014 | 40.6 | 1,814 | 400 | 292 | 653 |
| UNEMPLOYED | 744 | 5,239 | 17.5 | 285 | 192 | 181 | 85 |
| DISCOURAGED | 144 | 5,178 | 28.1 | 10 | 61 | 42 | 30 |
| LOW-PD FULL-EMP HEAD | 760 | 3,488 | 58.1 | 596 | --- | --- | 163 |
| OTHER LOW-EARN HEAD | 1,151 | 2,987 | 55.7 | 793 | --- | --- | 358 |
| EMP PART-TIME INVOL | 367 | 6,159 | 7.9 | 129 | 147 | 68 | 16 |
| EEI INDEX | 7.0% | --- | --- | 7.7% | 4.3% | 3.8% | 14.5% |

1968

### IN SMSA - BLACK

| | NUMBER (000) | TOTAL AVERAGE HOUSEHOLD INCOME | PERCENT POOR | FAMILY HEADS (000) | WIVES (000) | OTHER RELATIVES (000) | UNRELATED INDIVIDUALS (000) |
|---|---|---|---|---|---|---|---|
| TOTAL | 8,974 | $ 5,382 | 24.4 | 3,233 | 2,168 | 2,313 | 1,260 |
| IN LABOR FORCE | 5,723 | 6,189 | 16.4 | 2,512 | 1,138 | 1,229 | 843 |
| SUBEMPLOYED | 1,457 | 4,413 | 45.8 | 816 | 140 | 223 | 279 |
| UNEMPLOYED | 372 | 5,687 | 29.8 | 117 | 63 | 149 | 43 |
| DISCOURAGED | 66 | 5,465 | 21.0 | 9 | 23 | 5 | 29 |
| LOW-PD FULL-EMP HEAD | 443 | 4,641 | 49.8 | 393 | --- | --- | 50 |
| OTHER LOW-EARN HEAD | 398 | 2,786 | 73.8 | 256 | --- | --- | 142 |
| EMP PART-TIME INVOL | 179 | 6,255 | 16.5 | 41 | 53 | 69 | 16 |
| PERCENT SUBEMPLOYED | 25.5% | --- | --- | 32.5% | 12.3% | 18.1% | 33.1% |
| INADEQUATE EMP/EARN | 1,299 | 3,617 | 51.4 | 761 | 117 | 165 | 257 |
| UNEMPLOYED | 299 | 4,289 | 37.0 | 106 | 50 | 110 | 33 |
| DISCOURAGED | 55 | 3,903 | 25.1 | 9 | 23 | 0 | 23 |
| LOW-PD FULL-EMP HEAD | 416 | 4,132 | 53.0 | 368 | --- | --- | 48 |
| OTHER LOW-EARN HEAD | 386 | 2,422 | 76.1 | 244 | --- | --- | 142 |
| EMP PART-TIME INVOL | 143 | 5,133 | 20.6 | 34 | 43 | 55 | 11 |
| EEI INDEX | 22.7% | --- | --- | 30.3% | 10.2% | 13.4% | 30.5% |

1972

| MBER (000) | TOTAL AVERAGE HOUSEHOLD INCOME | PERCENT POOR | FAMILY HEADS (000) | WIVES (000) | OTHER RELATIVES (000) | UNRELATED INDIVIDUALS (000) |
|---|---|---|---|---|---|---|
| ,763 | $ 11,089 | 7.5 | 31,554 | 28,201 | 16,616 | 10,392 |
| ,834 | 12,668 | 4.4 | 26,231 | 11,450 | 9,148 | 6,005 |
| ,318 | 8,288 | 26.8 | 3,073 | 1,018 | 1,079 | 1,148 |
| ,339 | 10,833 | 12.5 | 778 | 555 | 712 | 293 |
| 282 | 10,181 | 15.6 | 45 | 147 | 79 | 12 |
| 786 | 5,445 | 52.5 | 657 | --- | --- | 129 |
| ,879 | 4,512 | 48.6 | 1,274 | --- | --- | 604 |
| ,033 | 11,972 | 3.1 | 319 | 317 | 288 | 110 |
| 12.0% | --- | --- | 11.7% | 8.9% | 11.8% | 19.1% |
| ,769 | 5,218 | 35.6 | 2,631 | 619 | 524 | 995 |
| ,492 | 6,608 | 19.7 | 586 | 359 | 338 | 208 |
| 192 | 6,504 | 22.9 | 45 | 72 | 62 | 12 |
| 711 | 4,221 | 58.1 | 585 | --- | --- | 126 |
| ,791 | 3,928 | 51.0 | 1,203 | --- | --- | 589 |
| 583 | 7,252 | 5.5 | 213 | 187 | 123 | 60 |
| 9.0% | --- | --- | 10.0% | 5.4% | 5.7% | 16.6% |

1972

| MBER (000) | TOTAL AVERAGE HOUSEHOLD INCOME | PERCENT POOR | FAMILY HEADS (000) | WIVES (000) | OTHER RELATIVES (000) | UNRELATED INDIVIDUALS (000) |
|---|---|---|---|---|---|---|
| ,847 | $ 7,008 | 23.0 | 3,932 | 2,438 | 2,943 | 1,534 |
| ,587 | 8,353 | 14.3 | 2,873 | 1,333 | 1,474 | 907 |
| ,706 | 5,907 | 43.0 | 892 | 177 | 367 | 270 |
| 618 | 6,978 | 30.1 | 188 | 108 | 234 | 88 |
| 120 | 5,287 | 65.9 | 33 | 29 | 58 | 0 |
| 330 | 6,906 | 47.2 | 299 | --- | --- | 31 |
| 459 | 3,850 | 63.1 | 329 | --- | --- | 130 |
| 180 | 7,534 | 13.0 | 43 | 40 | 76 | 22 |
| 25.9% | --- | --- | 31.0% | 13.3% | 24.9% | 29.8% |
| ,510 | 4,755 | 48.6 | 817 | 160 | 285 | 247 |
| 503 | 5,379 | 36.9 | 166 | 94 | 174 | 70 |
| 113 | 4,144 | 69.8 | 33 | 29 | 51 | 0 |
| 296 | 5,480 | 52.5 | 267 | --- | --- | 29 |
| 443 | 3,406 | 65.3 | 313 | --- | --- | 130 |
| 154 | 6,300 | 15.3 | 37 | 37 | 61 | 19 |
| 22.9% | --- | --- | 28.4% | 12.0% | 19.4% | 27.3% |

$740842175

1968

| NOT IN SMSA - WHITE | NUMBER (000) | TOTAL AVERAGE HOUSEHOLD INCOME | PERCENT POOR | FAMILY HEADS (000) | WIVES (000) | OTHER RELATIVES (000) | UNRELATED INDIVIDUAL (000) |
|---|---|---|---|---|---|---|---|
| TOTAL | 41,646 | $ 6,788 | 14.4 | 15,896 | 14,622 | 7,712 | 3,416 |
| IN LABOR FORCE | 24,266 | 7,765 | 8.8 | 13,027 | 5,807 | 3,804 | 1,629 |
| SUBEMPLOYED | 3,459 | 4,692 | 40.4 | 2,212 | 494 | 385 | 369 |
| UNEMPLOYED | 706 | 6,694 | 19.4 | 261 | 196 | 208 | 41 |
| DISCOURAGED | 149 | 4,493 | 34.7 | 19 | 88 | 28 | 14 |
| LOW-PD FULL-EMP HEAD | 1,142 | 3,660 | 54.7 | 1,047 | --- | --- | 95 |
| OTHER LOW-EARN HEAD | 926 | 3,224 | 57.1 | 729 | --- | --- | 196 |
| EMP PART-TIME INVOL | 536 | 7,125 | 10.2 | 156 | 210 | 149 | 22 |
| PERCENT SUBEMPLOYED | 14.3% | --- | --- | 17.0% | 8.5% | 10.1% | 22.6% |
| | | | | | | | |
| INADEQUATE EMP/EARN | 2,684 | 3,150 | 52.0 | 1,843 | 303 | 225 | 314 |
| UNEMPLOYED | 406 | 4,165 | 33.8 | 170 | 103 | 112 | 21 |
| DISCOURAGED | 125 | 3,085 | 41.4 | 14 | 73 | 23 | 14 |
| LOW-PD FULL-EMP HEAD | 1,014 | 2,855 | 61.6 | 921 | --- | --- | 93 |
| OTHER LOW-EARN HEAD | 827 | 2,557 | 63.9 | 647 | --- | --- | 180 |
| EMP PART-TIME INVOL | 313 | 4,634 | 17.5 | 91 | 127 | 89 | 6 |
| EEI INDEX | 11.1% | --- | --- | 14.1% | 5.2% | 5.9% | 19.3% |

1968

| NOT IN SMSA - BLACK | NUMBER (000) | TOTAL AVERAGE HOUSEHOLD INCOME | PERCENT POOR | FAMILY HEADS (000) | WIVES (000) | OTHER RELATIVES (000) | UNRELATED INDIVIDUAL (000) |
|---|---|---|---|---|---|---|---|
| TOTAL | 3,884 | $ 3,557 | 50.3 | 1,335 | 941 | 1,206 | 402 |
| IN LABOR FORCE | 2,269 | 4,152 | 40.3 | 981 | 470 | 594 | 224 |
| SUBEMPLOYED | 931 | 3,220 | 66.7 | 598 | 102 | 125 | 105 |
| UNEMPLOYED | 142 | 3,956 | 53.2 | 41 | 34 | 58 | 10 |
| DISCOURAGED | 59 | 2,010 | 76.7 | 26 | 12 | 15 | 6 |
| LOW-PD FULL-EMP HEAD | 343 | 3,526 | 65.2 | 316 | --- | --- | 28 |
| OTHER LOW-EARN HEAD | 269 | 2,493 | 79.3 | 209 | --- | --- | 60 |
| EMP PART-TIME INVOL | 118 | 4,165 | 53.6 | 7 | 56 | 52 | 2 |
| PERCENT SUBEMPLOYED | 41.0% | --- | --- | 61.0% | 21.7% | 21.1% | 47.0% |
| | | | | | | | |
| INADEQUATE EMP/EARN | 871 | 2,743 | 71.3 | 563 | 96 | 109 | 103 |
| UNEMPLOYED | 121 | 2,991 | 62.5 | 37 | 30 | 45 | 8 |
| DISCOURAGED | 59 | 2,010 | 76.7 | 26 | 12 | 15 | 6 |
| LOW-PD FULL-EMP HEAD | 319 | 2,975 | 70.0 | 292 | --- | --- | 28 |
| OTHER LOW-EARN HEAD | 262 | 2,318 | 81.3 | 202 | --- | --- | 60 |
| EMP PART-TIME INVOL | 109 | 3,548 | 57.7 | 6 | 54 | 48 | 1 |
| EEI INDEX | 38.4% | --- | --- | 57.4% | 20.5% | 18.3% | 45.8% |

1972

| NUMBER (000) | TOTAL AVERAGE HOUSEHOLD INCOME | PERCENT POOR | FAMILY HEADS (000) | WIVES (000) | OTHER RELATIVES (000) | UNRELATED INDIVIDUALS (000) |
|---|---|---|---|---|---|---|
| 40,336 | $ 8,803 | 13.3 | 15,194 | 14,009 | 7,420 | 3,714 |
| 23,655 | 10,242 | 8.2 | 12,114 | 5,885 | 3,992 | 1,665 |
| 3,859 | 6,792 | 33.5 | 2,300 | 633 | 515 | 411 |
| 1,072 | 9,631 | 15.9 | 410 | 287 | 319 | 56 |
| 206 | 6,761 | 23.0 | 43 | 104 | 39 | 19 |
| 977 | 4,938 | 51.5 | 910 | --- | --- | 67 |
| 1,039 | 4,344 | 50.6 | 801 | --- | --- | 238 |
| 565 | 9,804 | 8.4 | 136 | 242 | 157 | 30 |
| 16.3% | --- | --- | 19.0% | 10.7% | 12.9% | 24.7% |
| 2,845 | 4,246 | 45.5 | 1,889 | 376 | 234 | 347 |
| 592 | 5,578 | 28.8 | 262 | 169 | 135 | 27 |
| 139 | 3,706 | 34.0 | 38 | 70 | 16 | 14 |
| 858 | 3,773 | 58.7 | 792 | --- | --- | 66 |
| 957 | 3,586 | 54.9 | 725 | --- | --- | 232 |
| 299 | 5,923 | 15.8 | 71 | 137 | 82 | 8 |
| 12.0% | --- | --- | 15.6% | 6.4% | 5.9% | 20.8% |

1972

| NUMBER (000) | TOTAL AVERAGE HOUSEHOLD INCOME | PERCENT POOR | FAMILY HEADS (000) | WIVES (000) | OTHER RELATIVES (000) | UNRELATED INDIVIDUALS (000) |
|---|---|---|---|---|---|---|
| 3,595 | $ 4,961 | 42.6 | 1,190 | 834 | 1,228 | 343 |
| 2,084 | 5,900 | 30.5 | 831 | 431 | 634 | 188 |
| 794 | 4,980 | 54.4 | 459 | 68 | 183 | 84 |
| 149 | 6,364 | 40.0 | 39 | 32 | 70 | 8 |
| 84 | 5,377 | 50.1 | 5 | 5 | 64 | 10 |
| 212 | 5,352 | 59.2 | 198 | --- | --- | 14 |
| 249 | 3,668 | 67.8 | 205 | --- | --- | 45 |
| 100 | 6,673 | 36.1 | 13 | 31 | 48 | 7 |
| 38.1% | --- | --- | 55.3% | 15.8% | 28.9% | 44.6% |
| 675 | 3,905 | 64.0 | 409 | 46 | 141 | 80 |
| 110 | 4,446 | 54.4 | 33 | 18 | 51 | 7 |
| 71 | 4,215 | 59.2 | 5 | 0 | 57 | 10 |
| 188 | 4,414 | 67.0 | 173 | --- | --- | 14 |
| 236 | 3,222 | 71.5 | 192 | --- | --- | 45 |
| 71 | 4,984 | 51.0 | 6 | 27 | 33 | 4 |
| 32.4% | --- | --- | 49.2% | 10.6% | 22.2% | 42.4% |

**Library of Congress Cataloging in Publication Data**

Levitan, Sar A
    Employment and earnings inadequacy.

    (Policy studies in employment and welfare, no. 19)
    Includes bibliographical references.
    1. Labor supply—United States. 2. Unemployed—
United States. 3. Income—United States. 4. Index
numbers (Economics)   I. Taggart, Robert, 1945–
joint author.   II. Title.
HD5724.L42256      331.1'0973      74-6831
ISBN 0-8018-1623-8
ISBN 0-8018-1624-6 (pbk.)